A Black Woman's Worth!
My Queen and Backbone

Other Great Books by Dr. Dwayne L. Buckingham

Qualified, yet Single: Why Good Men Remain Single

Can Black Women Achieve Marital Satisfaction? How Childhood Nurturing Experiences Impact Marital Happiness

Unconditional Love: What Every Woman and Man Desires In A Relationship

A Black Man's Worth: Conqueror and Head of Household

Ground-Breaking Films by Dr. Dwayne L. Buckingham

A Black Man's Worth: Conqueror and Head of Household

A Black Woman's Worth: My Queen and Backbone

Qualified, yet Single: Why Good Men Remain Single

www.realhorizonsdlb.com

A Black Woman's Worth!
My Queen and Backbone

**R.E.A.L. for Strategies Preventing Burnout
and
Demoralization!**

Dr. Dwayne L. Buckingham, LCSW, BCD

**R.E.A.L. Horizons Consulting Service, LLC
Silver Spring, Maryland**

A Black Woman's Worth!
My Queen and Backbone

Unless otherwise indicated, all scripture quotations are taken from the King James Version of the Bible. In addition, any biographical information about Black women was taken from The Wikipedia, The Free Encyclopedia.

Additional copies of this book can be purchased on-line at www.realhorizonsdlb.com or by contacting:

R.E.A.L. Horizons Consulting Service, LLC
P.O. Box 2665
Silver Spring, MD 20915
240-242-4087 Voice mail

SECOND EDITION

Cover designed by Stephen Fortune

Library of Congress Control Number: 2011962623
Genre/Self-Help

ISBN: 978-0-9849423-1-2

Photos by Synica Tate

Printed in the United States of America

Dedication

To My Lord Jesus Christ, Who protects and
nurtures me daily.

To my beloved deceased mother, Arlene "Tot" Pettis, who
will always be my Queen!

And

To my nurturing sisters:
Linda, Alma, Cynthia and Bonnie

Thanks for the encouragement, support and unconditional love. Words cannot express my gratitude, but I will try. I wrote the poem on the next page to articulate my love and appreciation.

Thank You!

I am the Man that I am Because of you!

Thank you!

Life would be difficult without you!

Thank you!

Many women have entered and left my life, but not you!

Thank you!

At times I feel like giving up, but you never do!

Thank you!

Sharing my emotions is hard—however, I do, with you!

Thank you!

I can only hope to love like you!

Thank you!

You are a Queen and worthy of being treated like one, and I

Thank God for you!

Acknowledgments

I thank the following individuals who supported me as I journeyed into manhood and assisted me in understanding the worth of Black women.

Thelma Greene, you have a quiet persona, but a powerful presence.

Louise King, thanks for being a strong Black woman.

Eugenia Davis, thanks for opening up your heart and home.

Gloria Wright, you are one of the realest women I have ever met.

David Greene, thanks for teaching me how to survive and protect family.

Elisha Gregory, your devotion to family is notable. Thanks for caring.

Danielle Pettis, I love you, little brother. Thanks for having a big heart.

Jeffery Greene, you inspired me as a child. Thanks for being a leader.

Bennie Williams, you believed in me, and I love you for this.

Robert Milton, thanks for showing me how to stand by and support women.

Bettie and Ken Brakebill, thanks for extending loving hearts.

Linda and Bill Sodemann, thanks for not giving up on me.

Stacey Nichols, thanks for being you, and never stop being bighearted.

Keisha Milton, you have been a blessing. Thanks for being a positive woman.

Calvin Nelson, Jr. I appreciate your friendship. Thanks for being you.

Gladys Milton, thanks for accepting me into your heart and family.

Randall Smith, Jr., you inspire me to take that big step—marriage and fatherhood.

William Humphrey, thanks for being a positive friend.

Kevin Bonner, thanks for supporting me over the years.

LaNetra Kellar, I cherish your friendship and thank God for you.

Monica Stephenson, thanks for reintroducing me to Christ. You changed my life.

Bishop Ira Combs, Jr. I will always be grateful for the awesome spiritual guidance.

Pastor John K. Jenkins, Sr. I thank you and God for the life-changing sermons you give.

Thanks to every woman that influenced my life and made me who I am today.

Last but not least, I would like to give a special thanks to *Dr. Richard Chiles* for his guidance, support and wisdom. Thanks for being the father I never had.

Message to Black Women

I thank God for creating such a wonderful sisterhood—you. I pray that this book provides the tools to help you understand your worth and prevent burnout and demoralization. As Black women you have experienced and continue to experience hardships to which many cannot relate. I do not pretend to understand you or your hardships fully. However, I do know that you are the backbone of the Black community, and progress for us does not happen without you. I pledge to treat you like Queens, and I challenge you to continue our rich heritage by conducting yourselves like the Queens that you are. Your hardships are not in vain. On behalf of all Black men I am saying, "Sorry and thanks."

A Message to Single Black Women

I encourage you to position yourselves for marriage, but do not convince yourselves that you must be married or be in a relationship to feel whole or worthy of being treated like Queens. If you are not happy alone, you probably will not be happy with someone present. Establish a relationship with Christ and I assure you that you will feel whole and receive Queen Treatment.

Black on the Outside, Christian on the Inside

Life as a Christian is easier than Life as an African American.

As an African American, I struggle to find peace in this Sinful World, but as a Christian peace finds me.

As an African American, I am judged by my physical attributes, but as a Christian I am judged by the condition of my heart.

As an African American, I am consumed with feelings of bitterness, emptiness and discouragement, but as a Christian I am consumed with feelings of peacefulness, wholeness and hope.

As an African American, I am judged by the steps of my forefathers and mothers, but as a Christian I judged by the steps of my Lord and Savior.

As an African American, I am influenced by Worldly things, but as Christian I am influenced by Godly things.

As an African American, I have the potential to be a great spiritual leader like Dr. Martin Luther King, JR., but as a Christian I have the potential to nurture others and to lead like Jesus Christ.

As an African American, I struggle to connect with and love other ethnic groups, but as Christian connecting with and loving others come with ease.

As an African American, my image is tainted by negative labels such as hostile, aggressive, overbearing, and selfish, but as a Christian my image is illuminated by positive labels such as friendly, considerate, humble, and selfless.

As an African American, my life is influenced by capitalism, racism and violence, but as a Christian my life is influenced by helping the needy, loving thy neighbor and turning the other cheek.

As an African American, I cannot change my skin color nor do I desire to, but as a Christian I can change my attitude and must strive to.

As an African American, I despise diversity because some people use it to justify unruliness, but as Christian I celebrate diversity because it verifies God's creativity.

If I could embrace my role as a Christian as equally as I embrace my role as an African American, my life would be easier.

Diversity should be recognized as a means to celebrate God's creativity, not as a mean to justify unruliness.

- Dr. Dwayne L. Buckingham

Preface

While it is true that women were created as helpmates for men, Black women have been the backbone of the African American race throughout history. Their contributions, sacrifices, strong will and superb nurturing abilities have helped preserve the African American family and culture. As the saying goes, "Behind every strong Black man there is a strong Black woman." However, with the decline of strong Black men in the African American community, many Black women have taken on the double burden of providing for themselves and their children while also maintaining the home and rearing their children singlehandedly. This unfortunate phenomenon has caused many Black women to suffer from burnout, which, in turn, has contributed to the increase in demoralizing behavior exhibited by Black women and young girls.

In pursuit of economic and financial security, happiness, love and acceptance, many Black women and young girls have devalued their worth. Some engage in casual sex for money, popularity, peer approval, pleasure and/or excitement. Others enter into or remain in abusive or unhealthy relationships that are detrimental to their children, family, friends and themselves. These survival methods, unfortunately, prevent many Black women and young girls from developing healthy self-esteem, relationships, and, ultimately, a true understanding of their worth.

Every Black woman is unique; each woman copes with situations differently. What works for one Black woman might not work for the next. My aspiration to help my sisters understand their worth and prevent burnout and demoralization serves as the foundation for this book.

Are you suffering from burnout and/or engaging in demoralizing behavior? Burnout is a state of emotional and physical exhaustion caused by excessive and prolonged stress. People experiencing burnout often don't see any hope of positive change in their situations. Burnout can cause you to engage in behavior that is not consistent with your values or standard mode of performance. If you are suffering from burnout you might experience decreased interest, motivation, sensitivity, productivity and energy; increased hopelessness, powerlessness, cynicism and resentfulness. Burnout might also cause you to feel dull and mistrustful. Burnout can also cause demoralization: feelings of gloom and inadequacy due to engaging in activities that undermine your morals.

God inspired me to write and dedicate this book to all Black women and young girls who desire to understand their worth and regain control over their life. I am indebted to hundreds of women, both friends and family, who have impacted my life and helped me learn the value of a Black woman. I emptied my heart and soul into this book hoping that I can help you understand your worth. My goals are to convince you that you are a Queen and the backbone of the Black community and to provide you with R.E.A.L. strategies for preventing burnout and demoralization.

Contents

Introduction

Many Black women do not understand their worth. Why? Because in their day-to-day attempts to please and nurture others, feel loved, be happy, work and prosper, they do not make or have time to reflect on their worth. They often fail to understand that many of their day-to-day struggles are associated with not knowing and understanding their worth. Some women do not appreciate their current blessings because they are too preoccupied with focusing on what they lack.

God created woman to be a helpmate for man. He initially gave Adam and Eve equal dominion to care for the earth and to commune with him. Eve's worth was immeasurable. She was blessed to be the first female, had co-responsibility over creation and had a special relationship with God. Eve was created to be of one with Adam and to live eternally, enjoying an everlasting relationship with God. However, due to not understanding her worth and appreciating her blessings, Eve damaged her relationship with God. She allowed Satan to deceive her by distracting her from reflecting on her blessings, reminding her of what she did not have and tempting her with something she desired. Without seeking understanding or guidance from God or Adam, Eve did what Satan wanted. And to make matters worse, she shared her sin with Adam and blamed Satan for her indiscretion. This ill-fated disobedience that started with Eve and ended with Adam separated them from the Tree of Life and was the beginning of the fall of mankind.

The story of Adam and Eve clearly illustrates how easy it is to be deceived and do wrong when you lack knowledge and do not seek understanding or guidance. Satan was capable of deceiving Eve because she did not understand her worth, lacked knowledge and assumed that she could prosper by doing bad. Like Eve, many of you lack knowledge and/or understanding of your worth, thus making yourselves vulnerable and easy to deceive.

However, because of God's gift of Free Will, you have choices. You can stop reading this book and continue to be vulnerable to burnout, greed, sadness, hopelessness and anger, which will ultimately lead to demoralizing behavior. Or you can continue reading this book to gain a better understanding of your worth and learn to prevent burnout and demoralization. The choice is yours!

If you choose to continue reading, you will discover in the following chapters descriptions of common hardships experienced by Black women who do not know or seek to understand their worth. Seed Thoughts are presented at the beginning of each chapter to stimulate thinking. Each chapter includes a strategy for Black women and young girls to use to prevent burnout and demoralization. R.E.A.L. strategies are designed to empower you, but your ability to benefit from them will require you to have an open mind, positive attitude and desire to practice.

I think education is power. I think that being able to communicate with people is power. One of my main goals on this planet is to encourage people to empower themselves.

—*Oprah Winfrey*

Transformed by Knowledge and Wisdom

----------- *Chapter 1* -----------

As a young boy I did not understand the worth of a Black woman. I was not educated or informed. No man ever taught me to respect a Black woman or appreciate her. I grew up viewing women negatively. I thought all Black women were weak because they did things that nobody else would do and supported men who did not support them or stay with them. My mother birthed eight children and practically raised us by herself. She instilled the fear of God in us and taught us to be generous. She volunteered in church and gave to the needy. She did not have much money, but she would give money to other kids in the neighborhood. She was always willing to help someone else and did not ask for anything in return. She did it all. She worked long hours as a bricklayer to support my siblings and me. I remember having mixed feeling about my mother as a young child. I loved her wholeheartedly for taking care of me, but I was also angry with her. My siblings and I were often teased about not having a father present. We were also teased about my mother's employment status. I never understood why she chose to work as a bricklayer. I felt embarrassed and wanted her to get a "woman's job." I never expressed my emotions or concerns to my mother, and as a result, I never understood her.

At a young age I held a negative view of Black women. Witnessing the hardships and pain of my four sisters also compounded my ambivalence and negativity. They had children at early ages and engaged in activities similar to those of my mother: up-and-down relationships and raising their children alone. Only one of my sisters married, but this did not last long. Growing up and observing the hardships experienced by the women I cherished and loved was emotionally devastating. However, due to a lack of knowledge and respectful male role models, I grew up treating women the same way I saw men treat my mother and sisters.

As I entered my teenage years I engaged in casual sex and manipulated young girls to get what I wanted. I learned that girls from households similar to mine (single parent, abusive parent(s), strict parent(s), busy parent(s), etc.) often lacked knowledge about their worth and were searching for acceptance and love. I dated multiple young girls at the same time and capitalized on the fact that most of them lacked self-esteem. I continued this behavior throughout high school. My mode of operation, like that of other brothers, was to treat women as they treated themselves. If they acted irrationally, I treated them like irrational people. If they acted like whores, I treated them that way. If they showed too much emotion, I made them feel weak. Although I knew my actions were wrong, I treated females that way because they accepted it and I got my needs met. I did not feel guilty about my behavior, because it was "common."

The word "common" according to Webster's Dictionary is defined as belonging to or participated in by a community as a whole. Having no special distinction or quality; widely known or commonly encountered or ordinary. It was cool to have sex with multiple women and to dominate them. It defined manhood. At an early age I learned that people engaged in behaviors that were common to them regardless of whether they were right or wrong. People lived their lives according to the "survival of the fittest" concept, which justified unfair or mistreatment of those who were weak. This learned behavior can be attributed to societal and environmental influences. I guess I was a product of my environment. I could see the wrong in others' behavior, but I justified my own madness. For example, I treated young ladies harshly, but attempted to "knock" other brothers' heads off if they offended women in my family. I learned that common sense was not so common. I also learned that women think with their hearts and men think with both heads, which often leads to trouble. I must admit that I was one lost boy who was struggling to understand, love and respect Black women and myself. And to add to my emotional turmoil I lost the only woman I truly loved. My mother passed after my junior year in high school after suffering from brain cancer for a few months.

I never knew what it was like to feel lonely until I lost my mother. She was the only person who showed me love consistently, and I did not truly appreciate her greatness until she was gone. I learned that no one should be taken for granted and that life on earth is limited. However, my inability to bond with others continued. I did not understand why God took my mother from me while I was so young. I was robbed of my opportunity to share my emotions with her. I wanted to tell her that I loved her but was also angry with her. She exemplified qualities that I liked and did not like. She was strong and loved hard, but was often taken advantage of. I did not understand my mother and wanted to. I was frightened to go on living without her because I had become her. My heart/emotions dominated my thoughts and actions but these could not be expressed because of the pressure to look and act masculine. After all, to show emotions was a sign of weakness. This was confusing for me.

Many of us go through life trying to figure out who we are and make sense of our experiences, but unfortunately lack the basic *knowledge* and *wisdom* that are vital to understanding our experiences. Knowledge is information,

8

awareness, or understanding gained through experience or study. Wisdom is the ability to use knowledge and experience with common sense and insight. Insight is the experience of understanding or grasping the inner nature of things intuitively. I've learned that life experiences alone do not make a person wise. Individuals can go through life and experience things, but do not apply common sense or insight to address or solve their problems. Wisdom tells us how and when to use knowledge, but how does one cope with or solve hardships without proper knowledge and understanding?

My desire to develop an understanding of Black women and myself was challenging and at times seemed impossible. As I entered college my inability to bond with and understand Black women as well as myself continued, as reflected in this letter from my college female "friend":

Dear Dwayne,

You have a strong need for others to like and admire you. You worry about things more than you let on—even to your family and best friends. You have a tendency to be critical of yourself.

You pride yourself on being an independent thinker and do not accept others' opinions without satisfying proof. You have found it unwise to be too frank in revealing yourself to others. *I sense you are nursing a grudge against someone—probably a female—and you really should let go of that feeling.*

You are adaptable to social situations and your interests are very wide-ranging. At times you are extroverted and social; at other times you are introverted, wary and reserved. Some of your aspirations tend to be pretty unrealistic.

8

8

You feel things more keenly than most and because of this your feelings are often hurt by the thoughtless remarks of others.

As stated in the letter, I was an emotional wreck searching for answers. As I entered my sophomore year in college I decided to major in social work. I was determined to understand and learn about myself and Black women. I enrolled in numerous classes that focused on human behavior and development. As I studied, I began to acquire the knowledge that I so longed for. I learned about micro, mezzo and macro systems and how they interface. I also learned about child development, personality disorders and the psychological distress that occurs when a person or group of people are demoralized, exploited or oppressed. I was educated about Mary McLeod Bethune and other strong, resilient and prominent Black women. But, most important, I learned about philosophy, which is a universal science that considers the totality of reality and investigates the basic causes of all things; it examines the ultimate and absolute cause of all being. Philosophy primarily focuses on human activity, especially man's acts of knowing and doing. Philosophy means, literally, the love of wisdom and knowledge. Learning about philosophy helped me understand others' behaviors as well as my own.

I studied several philosophers, but was most drawn to the philosophies of Socrates and St. Augustine. Let's review Socrates' philosophy first. Socrates was committed to the pursuit of truth, linking knowing and doing to each other in such a way as to argue that "To know the good is to do the good." Socrates was curious about people's behavior. How does one do right? What guides one to do right? Are people influenced by external or internal sources? He attempted to answer these questions by studying the soul of humankind. The soul or psyche, according to Socrates, is the seat of rationality properly understood. He believed that the soul can either be good or bad, and that humankind's purpose is to make the soul as good as possible by not doing bad. This entails knowing that some things contradict others; for example, that love cannot mean hurting others. Through his thorough analysis of human rational abilities, he became convinced that people clearly understand right from wrong, but choose to engage in bad behavior because we think we are doing something good. To Socrates this was considered *ignorance*. He believed that people choose wrong out of ignorance, never for itself. I agree with Socrates and believe that we all have the ability to do right, but ignorance leads some of us to do what is wrong. Let's review some examples.

- Even though people know that stealing is bad, they do it because they believe that they can be rewarded in some way.

- A young woman is pregnant and does not know what to do, so she has an abortion, hoping that her life will be easier in some way. According to Socrates the young lady had an abortion because she was ignorant of the fact that killing another person could not make her life any easier because she failed to make her soul as good as possible.

Now let's review St. Augustine's Christian philosophy. He believed in God and wanted to develop a philosophy that would help him understand his faith. He believed that God was omniscient and omnipotent. St. Augustine believed that we acquire knowledge by reasoning. We learn that a thing cannot both be and not be at the same time. He searched for reasons. He believed that we acquire knowledge through our senses, but because our senses are limited and often deceive us, God enlightens our minds and enables us to obtain knowledge of eternal truth through illumination. God directs our mind upward to the highest level of knowledge, which is Him. The world reflects God's eternal thought, so to know one you must know the other.

Studying philosophy definitely helped me understand others and myself. I learned that people do bad things because they fail to gain correct knowledge about human nature and what it requires to do right and be happy. I also learned that God is the highest level of knowledge and we should always look upward. Acquiring knowledge through my **educational experience** was **the first step in my transformation** process.

In the early years of my profession as a clinical social worker, I gravitated toward and used two therapeutic approaches: cognitive therapy and the strengths-based approach. Cognitive therapy was developed and popularized by Albert Ellis and Aaron Beck. This approach in its most fundamental sense focuses on helping individuals identify irrational beliefs or distorted thinking that underlie unproductive behaviors. After irrational beliefs are identified, individuals are encouraged to replace them with rational beliefs that promote better functioning. In the strengths-based approach, strengths are identified and used to improve problems. This perspective focuses primarily on environmental and personal strengths.

To gain understanding and appreciation of a Black woman's worth and myself I used both approaches. Learning these modalities and applying them in my personal and professional life was very empowering. I learned how to connect with and help others by maintaining positive thoughts and focusing on individuals' strengths. Although I realize that social, economic and political injustice exists and "brothers need to step up to the plate," I firmly believe that our ability to cope with our hardships comes from within. Each one of us matters and can make a difference by equipping ourselves with proper knowledge.

Through a combination of personal, educational and professional experiences, I acquired knowledge about human behavior that increased my appreciation for Black women forever. Let's review:

- Birthed and raised by a single Black Woman
- Witnessed the hardships and pain of four sisters
- Dated XXX number of Black Women
- Acquired two degrees in human behavior and development
- Received two clinical licenses and board certification
- Provided cognitive therapy to over 2000 Black Women

Acquiring knowledge through my **professional experience and combining it with my educational experience** completed **the second step in my transformation** process. I was pleased with how my transformation was progressing, and I thought I had obtained sufficient *knowledge* to *totally* understand Black women and myself. I was wise enough to apply my educational knowledge to help others profession- ally. However, I continued to struggle personally. I asked myself, why do I continue to struggle with this issue, even after I have prepared myself accordingly? To find answers to resolve my struggle I reflected on childhood teachings from my mother. In my childhood she would tell me to pray and ask God for insight and guidance. She was not an educated woman, but she was smart enough to know where to find peace and understanding. She was firm in her stance that my siblings and I must have a relationship with God and attend church. I never understood why she placed so much emphasis on having a relationship with God. I watched others mistreat her. She would somehow find it in her heart to forgive them. I viewed her behavior as weakness.

To develop an understanding of this behavior and resolve my struggle, I decided to establish a relationship with God for myself. Through fellowship with other Christians and excellent teaching from superb pastors, I learned the importance of having a relationship with God. As St. Augustine stated, "To know the world you must know God." I began to study the Bible and attend church and Bible study weekly. As I studied the *Word* I learned why my mother insisted that all of her children have a relationship with God. The scripture says, "Train up a child in the way he should go: and when he is old, he will not depart from it" (Proverbs 22:6). My Christian experience taught me that God's *Word* is the highest level of knowledge that can be obtained. As a result of my spiritual growth and basic understanding of the *Word*, I also learned that nothing makes sense without God. Life has no meaning without the *Word* and our senses can only provide limited knowledge and wisdom. Therefore, we must ask God for wisdom and he will enlighten us. "If any of you lack wisdom, let him ask of God, that giveth to all men liberally, and upbraideth not; and it shall be given him" (James 1:5). "Wisdom is the principal thing: therefore get wisdom: and with all thy getting get understanding" (Proverbs 4:7).

Through my Christian experience God blessed me with knowledge and wisdom that enhanced my understanding of my mother's worth and behavior. She conducted herself like a Queen because God's Word ordered her to. She was not perfect, but she attempted to live righteously. I learned that it is my responsibility to cherish, respect and treat all women like Queens regardless of my understanding of them. I also learned that I will not always understand women or life's hardships, but the Word teaches me: "Trust in the LORD with all thine heart; and lean not unto thine own understanding. In all thy ways acknowledge him, and he shall direct thy paths" (Proverbs 3:5-6). I believe that education is very important and our personal and professional experiences can provide some knowledge and wisdom. However, until we learn to live by the *Word*, we will continue to experience unnecessary hardships. With this profound understanding I successfully completed the **final step of my transformation** by **integrating** and **applying** my **personal, educational, professional and Christian teachings and experiences** into my daily life.

As a result of acquiring proper knowledge and wisdom I transformed from being a lost, disturbed, disrespectful, unappreciative boy to a thoughtful, caring, spiritual and generous man who now understands and appreciates your worth. "When I was a child, I spoke as a child, I understood as a child, I thought as a child; but when I became a man, I put away childish things" (1 Corinthians 13:11). I thank God for my transformation and pray that this book establishes the foundation for your transformation.

Questions for Reflection and Discussion

Do you consider yourself to be knowledgeable?
Yes____ No_____ (Explain)

Do you consider yourself to be wise?
Yes____ No_____ (Explain)

Can you have knowledge without wisdom?
Yes____ No_____ (Explain)

What is knowledge and how is it acquired?

What is the highest level of knowledge you can obtain?

Are knowledge and wisdom the same?
Yes____ No_____ (Explain)

Use the space below to record your feelings and/or thoughts about this chapter. What did you learn?

*Notes*_____

_____
_____
_____
_____
_____
_____
_____
_____
_____
_____
_____
_____
_____
_____
_____
_____
_____
_____
_____
_____
_____
_____
_____
_____
_____
_____

Women, if the soul of the nation is to be saved, I believe that you must become its soul.

—*Coretta Scott King*

Keep it "R.E.A.L."

----------------------A Black Woman's Worth!----------------------

----------- *Chapter 2* -----------

REAL: Implies authenticity, genuineness, or factuality. Many Blacks use the phrase "Keep it REAL" to encourage each other to be genuine and authentic, not fake: having a false or misleading appearance. As a member of the Black community I was often told not to pretend to be something or someone I was not. I was told to be true to myself and others, but to always *"keep it REAL."* I decided to talk to you about this motto because I feel that it has contributed to low self-esteem and has caused many Blacks, especially Black women, to engage in self-destructive or self-inhibiting behavior. Here are a few examples of how the motto is most commonly used in the Black community:

- Don't be a sellout, keep it REAL!
- Don't date outside your race, keep it REAL!
- Don't snitch, keep it REAL!

Can I talk to you about this motto? I do not understand why, as a race of people who have been oppressed, restricted and depersonalized, we continue to place limitations on ourselves. Let's review each phrase to better understand how it can lead to self-inhibiting or self-destructive behavior.

"Don't be a sellout, keep it REAL" is often used to remind us to maintain our Blackness. "Do not give into White America." "Keep it 'hood." As Blacks enter the main-stream, many struggle with this. Securing a nice home, a car or other items, in addition to status, often creates mixed feelings. Many feel a sense of accomplishment and pride and at the same time feel the pressure of "keeping it REAL." They minimize or reduce their accomplishments to fit in. They feel guilty about their success and sometimes fail to meet their full potential. I personally do not understand why we do not support and uplift each other instead of creating separation. If you make it in the mainstream, you are not completely accepted by Blacks who do not. I think this phrase divides us and prevents Blacks from progressing. Stop player hating and use that energy to capitalize on your God-given strengths. Show your brother or sister some love instead of knocking them down. Believe me, it is needed.

"Don't date outside your race, keep it REAL" is used to encourage us to date other Blacks exclusively. I really struggle with this, especially when I hear children of God say it. As a brother I definitely prefer to have a sister by my side, but as I have grown in my walk with God I have realized that love does not come in colors. So often we restrict our emotions and wonder why we can't find love. I have spent the past five years looking for a sister to grow old with. However, I have decided not to limit myself anymore, and I do not think you should limit to whom you give your heart, either. I am all about building up the Black community and having a sister by my side, but limiting myself is no longer an option. I pray that God sends me a Queen, but until He does, my heart is open. I encourage you to open your hearts as well.

"Don't snitch, keep it REAL" is used to encourage us to withhold information. I have seen several Blacks use this motto in a self-destructive manner. My nephew is currently serving a life sentence for a crime he committed with others. He received the longest sentence because he did not snitch—and, unfortunately, his partners in crime did. Withholding information got him life in prison. This example is extreme, but situations like this happen daily.

In my opinion, the "keep it REAL" motto has created emotional distress and confusion for many Blacks. I have personally witnessed some of you engaging in demoralizing or self-inhibiting behavior in an attempt to *"keep it REAL."* For example: having sex with multiple guys because you were dared and teased about not keeping it REAL; remaining in abusive/degrading relationships because you were trying to keep it REAL; and refusing to date outside your race because you were keeping it REAL. This unselfish commitment to be genuine to others, especially members of the Black community, can prove detrimental to your emotional and physical health.

Many of you have a profound need to hear the truth and will often accept and tolerate "crap" as long as you are not lied to. I have heard some Black women say they would engage in demoralizing behavior such as dating a married man as long as they know up front: "I would date a married man if he tells me he is married up front. As long as he *keeps it REAL* we are good. Girl, I know he is a dog, but he *keeps it REAL*." I have also heard brothers say they can have sex and relationships with multiple Black women as long as they *keep it REAL*: "I'm kicking it with someone now, but I really like you. I am just being up front with you. I like you so I am *keeping it REAL*." How many of you have found yourself in similar situations? Why do you accept or tolerate such behavior? What does *keeping it REAL* mean to you? Will you shame yourself to *keep it REAL*? I am not knocking any woman or man for *keeping it REAL*, but I challenge you to think about the potential harsh consequences of *keeping it REAL*. **If keeping it REAL means to be genuine and authentic, how can someone love you and disrespect you at the same time?** Is that *keeping it REAL* or being Fake? Why are you so concerned about pleasing others? Why do you continue to engage in demoralizing behavior if you know right from wrong? Is keeping it REAL that important?

You can keep it REAL and not demoralize or burn yourself out. If you live by the *"Keep it REAL"* motto, make sure it benefits you in a healthy manner. To help you apply the motto in a productive way, I formulated an uplifting and heartfelt concept. Throughout the following chapters, REAL is spelled "R.E.A.L." It is written in this manner to help you grasp the concept below.

The *"R"* encourages you to approach situations in a **Realistic** manner. It is important to express an awareness of things as they really are, but I encourage you to use sound judgment and demonstrate empathy. I also encourage you to seek to understand the source of problems before you attempt to address or solve them.

The *"E"* encourages you to exercise sound reasoning in order to develop rational **Expectations** or beliefs. The expectations you have of yourself, others and life in general often reflect how you live your life. Eliminate irrational expectations and replace them with rational ones.

The *"A"* encourages you to maintain a positive **Attitude** and image of yourself and others. Do not let your attitude or feeling prevent you from being happy or progressing in life. Negativity begets negativity. Change starts with you.

The *"L"* encourages you to develop unconditional **Love** for yourself and others. Establish a deep, tender, indefinable feeling of affection and attentiveness toward yourself and others that is not determined or influenced by someone or something.

I developed this concept with the hope that it will inspire you to apply it in your life. I have personally used it and know the benefits. God's purpose for us is to make our souls as good as possible and to live healthy productive lives by doing right. I am simply asking you to keep it R.E.A.L. as you do what God desires. I challenge you to practice this concept daily and be flexible in your thinking as you continue reading. Keep it R.E.A.L.—***Don't Stop Now!***

Questions for Reflection and Discussion

Do you engage in self-destructive or self-inhibiting behavior?

Why do you engage in and/or tolerate such behavior?

What does "Keep it REAL" mean to you?

Will you shame yourself to "keep it REAL"?

Can you apply the R.E.A.L. concept in your life? (Explain)

Use the space below to record your feelings and/or thoughts about this chapter. What did you learn?

*Notes*_____

_____
_____
_____
_____
_____
_____
_____
_____
_____
_____
_____
_____
_____
_____
_____
_____
_____
_____
_____
_____
_____
_____
_____
_____
_____
_____
_____
_____
_____
_____
_____

For I am my mother's daughter, and the drums of Africa still beat in my heart. They will not let me rest while there is a single Negro boy or girl without a chance to prove his worth.

—Mary McLeod Bethune

Be Realistic

----------- *Chapter 3* -----------

Many of you believe that you can build a stable home without a solid foundation and the proper tools. Some of you feel comfortable knowing that your foundation is shaky and your toolbox is not properly stocked, while others are too busy to seek the proper tools. Nevertheless, you continue to build your home. And after years of despair, anger, pain and frustration, you decide to restock your toolbox. You pamper yourself with clothes, trips and/or other insignificant luxuries to feel better. However, you fail to address your foundational issues. Like a rocking chair you continue to move, but make no progress.

The process of building a home is similar to that of understanding your worth. There are several procedures that you must perform to ensure that your home will be stable. First, and most important, is the ability to stabilize the foundation. If the foundation is not stabilized properly the home will eventually collapse. However, to stabilize the foundation properly you must understand what is required to make the foundation strong. A wise woman realizes that she cannot fix a problem unless she understands and addresses the root cause.

Understanding Your Worth

God equipped you with gifts that astonish men. A woman is capable of giving life to the world, comforting the sick, giving moral support, showing compassion, loving unconditionally, standing up against injustice, bearing hardships, carrying burdens, and holding happiness, love and joy. A woman shares in the image of God.

As a Black woman it is important to understand your worth. Your happiness and prosperity begin and end with your understanding. A woman who does not understand her significance positions herself to be used for others' gain. Undoubtedly, you are God's most *versatile* creation. However, your inability and/or unwillingness to understand your worth also make you God's most *vulnerable* creation.

Too often, you fail to surrender time to reflect and learn about yourself and those who came before you. Unfortunately, this selfless but neglectful behavior often causes unnecessary suffering. To understand your worth and regain control over your life, you must first understand where you came from. As James Baldwin so elegantly stated, "If you are not afraid to look back, nothing you are facing can frighten you."

Learn your Heritage

Throughout history Black women have played an instrumental role in determining the fate of mankind, especially African Americans. Time has proven that women who understand their worth possess the ability to control their destiny, influence others, negotiate peace and comfort those in need. However, time has also proven that women can cause significant pain for themselves and others if they lack understanding of their worth.

Assumptions regarding your worth stem from your actions as well as those of others. Defining your worth based on the actions and views of others can be both beneficial and detrimental.

Selecting women after whom to model your life is important. Modeling your life after women who degrade and devalue themselves can prove detrimental to the development of a healthy sense of self-worth. Search for women you respect and admire. It is important to look for women who exhibit qualities that are uplifting and inspiring. Seeking guidance from wise women can help you understand yourself and provide safety. Proverbs 11:14 says, "Where no counsel is, the people fall: but in the multitude of counselors there is safety." Some of you do not have to search far or hard for a role model or counselor. You might have women in your life such as your mother, grandmother, aunt, sister, friend or teacher who exhibit the qualities you desire to exemplify. However, if you struggle to identify with someone, remember that your heritage is rich with women who were self-confident and knew their worth. Women like Harriet Tubman, Sojourner Truth, Mary McLeod Bethune, Madame C. J. Walker, Mary Ann Shadd, Ida Wells-Barnett and Fannie Lou Hamer made significant contributions to the African American race and inspired many people while doing so.

Learning about our heritage can help you appreciate your worth. The women mentioned above were often referred to as Queens! Why? To increase your understanding of their worth I would like you to join me on a journey down heritage lane. While on our journey we will take a look at their:

- **Contributions;**
- **Powerful speaking ability;**
- **Superb nurturing ability;**
- **Powerful presence;**
- **Independent spirit; and**
- **Sacrifices.**

Women and young girls who go through life not knowing their worth are at greater risk for burnout and demoralization. Keep an open mind as we journey down heritage lane to review the qualities you inherited from our ancestors. The ability to enhance your understanding of your worth begins with you, but I will accompany you to demonstrate my support and appreciation. Below are a few quotations that are intended to inspire you as we embark on our journey.

Seek to learn and understand your heritage to gain a deeper understanding of your worth.
—Dwayne L. Buckingham

It is not the strongest of species that survives, nor the most intelligent, but rather the one most adaptable to change!
—Charles Darwin

I am where I am because of the bridges that I crossed. Sojourner Truth was a bridge. Harriet Tubman was a bridge. Ida B. Wells was a bridge. Madame C. J. Walker was a bridge. Fannie Lou Hamer was a bridge.
—Oprah Winfrey

Embarking on this journey will be one of the most rewarding things you will do as a Black woman. As we reflect on our past, you may experience mixed emotions: happiness and anger; sadness and joy, but at the end of our journey I promise you will be inspired. Hold your breath and get ready for the escapade that will change your view of yourself forever. Are you ready? Let's go. We'll start our journey by reviewing our ancestors' contributions.

Harriet Tubman was an abolitionist, Civil War soldier, and women's rights advocate. She was born in Maryland in 1821. Like many slaves, she could not read or write and was beaten regularly by her owners. As a child she sustained a severe head injury as a result of intentionally blocking the path of an overseer who was pursuing another slave. This early act of bravery caused her to be ill for years and she never fully recovered. Tubman was definitely a fighter. She was not willing to accept her misfortunate or allow others to control her. This exceptional Black woman left her brothers and husband to escape to freedom, and later led more than 300 other slaves North and to Canada to their freedom. Tubman was known as the best conductor on the Under-round Railroad and was one of the best social reformers and abolitionists of her time. She was a superb advocate who spoke against slavery and fought for women's rights until her death in 1913.

After learning about Ms. Tubman I was overwhelmed with joy and pride. Tubman was not a selfish woman. She risked her life and freedom to help others. She went back. She was caring, thoughtful, nurturing, resilient and hopeful. Her devotion and contribution earned her the ultimate honor of being buried with full military honors.

From Ms. Tubman's life I learned that fear can enslave us, but courage can free us. I also learned that we have choices in life and we control our destiny. What did you learn?

Mary Ann Shadd, was born in 1823 to Harriet and Abraham Shadd. She was the eldest of thirteen children. Shadd grew up watching her family fight for the freedom of slaves. Her father was instrumental in the Underground Railroad operation and worked for William Lloyd Garrison's *Liberator.* Influenced by her family's efforts, Shadd joined the fight against slavery and eventually became the first Black Woman editor in North America.

She used her gift of writing to attract readers to the issues surrounding slavery and exploitation of free Blacks.

Shadd wrote articles that educated the general public about the cruelty of slavery. She preached against individuals who took advantage of freed slaves and attempted to teach slaves how to be self-sufficient. She was committed to helping slaves, but was forced to migrate to Canada with her brother after the passing of the Fugitive Slave Law in 1850.

In Canada, she was very active. She founded a racially integrated school with the support of the American Missionary Association. Shadd continued her crusade against those who did not teach Blacks how to be self-sufficient. In 1853 she founded the *Provincial Freeman Newspaper* to promote moral reform and civil rights for Blacks.

Shadd advocated for Blacks for many years and used her newspaper as her voice until the newspaper declined; she moved to Washington, D.C. and served as a recruiting officer for the Union Army, promoting Black Nationalism. While in Washington, she also established a school for Black children, attended Howard University Law School and became the first Black female lawyer in the United States.

Shadd used her extraordinary writing skill to speak against slavery. She did not resort to violence or belittle herself to get her point across. She believed that she could make a difference and fought against injustice wherever it existed. She was caring, thoughtful, nurturing, resilient and hopeful.

Shadd was all about self-reliance. She did not believe that Blacks would ever be free until they learned to fend for themselves. She was adventurous and brave. Shadd supported the idea of changing yourself if you could not change the environment and I learned that acquiring knowledge is the first step to self-reliance. I also learned that giving back is fundamental. What did you learn?

---------------------Be Realistic----------------------

How are you feeling? Don't Exhale yet. We have only completed the first step of our journey. Now let's review our ancestors' powerful speaking ability.

Sojourner Truth, was born Isabella Baumfree in 1797 and later became one of the most prominent national speakers on human rights for slaves and women. However, like Tubman she did not have an easy life. As a child she only spoke Dutch and was beaten frequently due to miscommunication with her masters. To cope with the severe abuse she found a safe haven in religion. She prayed out loud. Baumfree was sold frequently and denied the right to select her husband. At the demand of her master she married a slave with whom she was not in love and birthed four children. After experiencing years of abuse at the hands of her master, Baumfree fled with a daughter and left her other three children behind. And due to God's Divine intervention she was blessed to find a home with slave owners who treated her as a human. This experience contributed to her spiritual rebirth that inspired her to preach. She attended church often and eventually became known as an outstanding preacher with phenomenal influence.

In 1829, she helped form a utopian community called "The Kingdom" at Sing Sing, New York, which was soon disbanded following the murder of its leader. Baumfree was implicated but not charged, and relocated to New York City.

After losing all she had acquired and experiencing a spiritual undertaking, Baumfree changed her name to Sojourner Truth to signify her new role as a traveler telling the truth about slavery. She set out traveling East in 1843 to accomplish this. Her popularity grew, and in 1864 she was invited to the White House where she was greeted by President Lincoln. Truth later served as a counselor for the National Freedman's Relief Association.

Ms. Truth was undeniably a go getter. She found refuge in religion and used spirituality to cope with life challenges. She was committed to telling the truth and used her God-given talent to accomplish her goal. She was caring, thoughtful, nurturing, resilient and hopeful. Her dedication to serving and speaking on behalf of others led to a self-fulfilling life.

From Truth's life I learned that the truth cannot be denied and respect is earned by demanding it and returning it as you acquire it. What did you learn? Are you inspired yet? If no, relax and tighten your seatbelt as we review the superb nurturing ability our ancestors exemplified.

Ida Wells-Barnett, born in 1862 was a natural caregiver. At the young age of sixteen she took on the responsibility of raising her siblings after the unfortunate death of her parents to smallpox. Barnett's giving spirit did not go unnoticed. With support from members in the Black community, she earned a college degree from Rust College. After completing college she worked as a teacher. Barnett was fortunate to have an education, but she was not exempt from racism. In 1884, she was forcefully moved from a segregated coach while traveling to Nashville. Barnett did not tolerate unfair treatment and eventually sued the railroad. She was awarded a $500 settlement.

As a journalist, speaker and part owner of the *Memphis Free Speech and Headlight*, Barnett consistently wrote about the poor conditions of Black children in local schools. Known for her thoughtfulness, she began an anti-lynching campaign in 1892 after three of her close friends were lynched by a mob. Barnett was also one of two Black women to sign the call for the formation of the NAACP. In addition, she founded the Negro Fellowship League and served as its president.

Blessed with a nurturing and considerate heart, Barnett risked her life to advocate for justice. Helping others appeared to come naturally for her. She was caring, thoughtful, nurturing, resilient and hopeful. This outspoken philanthropist inspired me to advocate for those who cannot advocate for themselves. I learned to speak against injustice and to help those who are not as fortunate as myself. What did you learn? Take a deep breath, but do not Exhale. You are doing well and we will successfully complete this journey, but not before we review how our ancestors made their presence known. Are you ready?

Mary McLeod Bethune was born a slave in Mayesville, South Carolina in 1875 before emancipation. She was the fifteenth of seventeen children. In her childhood she picked cotton and attended a Methodist mission school. As an adult Bethune was committed to advancing the African American race by promoting and establishing equal educational opportunities. She opened the Daytona Normal Industrial Institute, now known as the Bethune–Cookman College in 1904. The institution was established to educate Negro girls. Bethune served as president at the institution for several years before taking on more aggressive roles in the Black community and throughout the nation.

Bethune served in several capacities during Franklin D. Roosevelt's administration, including head of the Division of Negro Affairs of the National Youth Administration and advisor on selecting officer candidates for the Women's Army Corps. Bethune set the bar high for African Americans, both male and female, during her life time. She founded the National Council of Negro Women, served as president of the Association for the Study of Negro Life and History, vice-president of the NAACP, and received the Haitian Medal of Honor and Merit, the country's highest honor.

Ms. Bethune was a breath of fresh air for many African Americans. She was well respected and honored because she equipped herself and others with knowledge. She believed that every Black child had an inherited birthright to a good education. She was caring, thoughtful, nurturing, resilient and hopeful. Bethune provided hope and took pride in helping others excel.

She was living proof that knowledge was the key to opening doors and enhancing an individual's ability to succeed. I learned that status does not determine your destiny—you do. I also learned that knowledge is power. What did you learn? Take a moment or two to meditate on what you have already read before we move on. Learn to reflect before you take action. This simple task will enable you to appreciate your blessings. Are you being blessed? If yes, let's continue.

As you and I both know, a large percentage of our ancestors did not have much and were not expected to achieve economic stability. However, there was and is an exception to every rule and Madam C. J. Walker was that exception. She embodied the independent spirit that led to her financial stability.

Madam C. J. Walker, was born Sarah Breedlove on a Delta, LA cotton plantation in 1867. She was considered to be the first Black American woman millionaire. However, Walker did not reach millionaire status without some hardships. She was orphaned at age seven, married at age 14 and widowed with a two year old daughter. After the loss of her husband she relocated to St. Louis, MO where she lived with family members and earned $1.50 daily doing laundry. Walker was driven. She did not allow her social or economic status to prevent her or her daughter from progressing. She saved enough money to send her daughter to college. Walker was born with a survival and an entrepreneurial spirit. With less than two dollars in her possession, she decided to establish her own line of hair-care products in 1906. With the assistance of her husband, Walker established a mail-order business in Denver, Colorado and her business blossomed to include a beauty school in Pittsburgh. Several years later, she had established offices in Indianapolis and Harlem. Walker's visionary skills contributed to the company's growth and by 1916 the company had thousands of employees, both men and women, in the U.S., Central America, and the Caribbean.

Walker was known for giving to and helping all African Americans, but was specifically concerned with helping Black women achieve economic independence. Her business philosophy was centered on helping Black women achieve economic independence. She encouraged Black women to pursue opportunities instead of sitting around and waiting. Walker used her financial status and social influence to promote fair and equitable economic rights for Blacks and for all women.

Walker possessed superb business skills that were not common during her time. Her creativity and ability to see beyond her current situation led to an empire. She dreamed and worked hard to make it come true. She exemplified strength and was inducted into the Women's Hall of Fame in 1993. She was caring, thoughtful, nurturing, resilient and hopeful.

Walker taught Blacks that waiting will get you nowhere, but hard work, patience and persistence will succeed. I learned that creative and independent thinking can be beneficial. What did you learn?

As we near the end of our journey, I would like to commend you for taking the time to accompany me. I never doubted that you would complete the journey. However, I do know that your time is valuable. But with patience and sacrifice comes rewards. In my short time on this earth I have learned to be patient and have made a few sacrifices that benefited others as well as myself. I felt good about my sacrifices and even bragged and boasted about them to others. However, after I read and learned about Fannie Lou Hamer I quickly humbled myself. She sacrificed for the well-being of all. Let's explore what she did.

Fannie Lou Hamer, born in 1917 was a civil rights activist and leader who was known for her key role in organizing the Mississippi Freedom Summer for the Student Nonviolent Coordinating Committee (SNCC) and serving as Vice-Chair of the Mississippi Freedom Democratic Party. Hamer was also known as a pleasant and spiritual woman who astonished people with her amazing speaking ability and unmatched commitment to civil rights. Hamer was motivated by her Biblical belief in justice. She inspired others with Christian hymns such as "Go Tell on the Mountain" and "This Little Light of Mine." She fought for voting rights for Blacks and founded the Mississippi Freedom Democratic Party because the Democratic Party of Mississippi did not permit Blacks. Hamer was successful in her activist role, but her success did not come without sacrifice. Her sacrifice started at an early age. Hamer was not born with a silver spoon in her mouth. In fact, her parents were sharecroppers and worked very hard to take care of Hamer, who was the youngest of twenty children. Like many youth during that era, she was forced to leave school to help support her family.

Sacrificing appeared to be part of Hamer's character make up. She was the first person to volunteer to vote despite serious threatens of violence. During her early activism years she was harassed by the police, lost her job and received death threats from the KKK. She was even arrested and beaten brutally by the police after attending an activist event in South Carolina. This severe beating at the hands of law enforcement did not stop Hamer from organizing voter registration drives after returning to Mississippi.

Hamer was a winner in all aspects of life. She sacrificed and completed life's race with her head held high. She coined the phrase, "I am sick and tired of being sick and tired." But most importantly, she took action to cope with and solve her frustration. She was caring, thoughtful, nurturing, resilient and hopeful. Hamer was and still is a true inspiration to many Blacks. In learning about Hamer, I learned the importance of voting and expressing my freedom of speech to challenge injustice. What did you learn?

Now that we have completed our journey, do you have a greater understanding of our heritage and your worth? Before you answer, Exhale. Are you convinced that our ancestors knew and understood their worth? They gave back, used their God-given talents, did not settle for less and never stopped being hopeful. Despite their hardships, they succeeded. They defined strength, endurance and resiliency. They conducted themselves like Queens. They were self-governing, supreme leaders who respected themselves and gained the respect of others.

I hope I have helped you understand why our ancestors were significant and often referred to as Queens. According to the Free Dictionary Thesaurus, a Queen is "Something personified as a woman who is considered the best or most important of her kind. A person who represents an abstract quality; she is the personification of optimism." I am convinced that our ancestors met all the qualifications to be considered Queens. Do you agree? How do you view yourself? Can you answer the following questions:

- Do you consider yourself to be a queen?
- Do you believe that you are the best or most important of your kind?

- Do you represent an abstract quality? A quality that is difficult to describe that is unique to you.
- Are you the personification of optimism? Are you a woman who embodies hope?
- Do you possess traits Queens exemplify: supreme and self-governing.
- Have you gained the respect of others?

Our ancestors were the backbone of their communities. Like many of you, they worked and took care of others without devaluing themselves. Are you the backbone of your community? Can you carry the torch? Hopefully you are not offended by my questions. I do not intend to imply that you are responsible for the plight of the African American race, but I do want you to understand your worth. If the backbone malfunctions the rest of the body does not function properly.

Like our ancestors, you are a Queen and the backbone of the Black community. You inherited the traits, talents, and optimistic attitude of our ancestors, and you are capable of accomplishing whatever you desire when you understand your worth. A woman who knows her worth accepts herself as she is, including the God-given qualities that make her unique. She chooses her own goals and values and lives by her own choice. She does not allow others to dictate her life.

If you are not capable of changing your situation, you can change your state of mind. Our ancestors did not allow their financial, social, emotional or economic status to deter them from living righteously and making a difference. They valued themselves, people, equality and freedom. They expected and demanded to be treated fairly and with respect. They maintained their worth and dignity while getting their needs met.

Despite hardships they faced, they never stop believing that they were worthy. Whatever their hearts desired, they fought for it and succeed with dignity. I encourage you to adopt and model their behavior and attitudes. Black women like, Rosa Parks, Coretta Scott King, Maya Angelou, Carol Moseley Braun, Oprah Winfrey and Condoleeza Rice honored our ancestors by adopting their behavior and attitudes while also elevating Blacks to another level. Like our ancestors they understood their worth. Let's briefly review their accomplishments.

Rosa Parks, born in 1913 was a hard working woman who held several jobs to provide for her younger brother and herself. But on December 1, 1955, her life changed. After working extremely hard, she boarded a bus heading home. As the bus filled to capacity seating became scarce. During this period Blacks were expected to relinquish their seats to Whites if warranted according to segregation laws. A White person boarded the bus and Parks was asked to give up her seat. Tired and fed up, she refused and was arrested for violating Alabama's segregation laws. Outraged and sick and tired of being sick and tired, the Black community launched a bus boycott that lasted 381 days.

Parks along with Dr. Martin Luther King, Jr. and other Blacks fought back and their actions dismantled segregation on Montgomery's buses. Parks later served as secretary of the Montgomery, Alabama NAACP chapter and continued her commitment to civil rights until her death in 2005.

Coretta Scott King, born in 1927 was a woman who gave up her dream of being a musician to support her husband, Dr. Martin Luther King, Jr. Ms. King married Dr. King in 1953 and later birthed four children. Coretta understood and supported her husband. She stood by Dr. King's side as the Montgomery bus boycott began and stood even stronger after her home was bombed. Coretta provided a first-hand lesson to women who did not know how to support their men. She marched side by side with Dr. King and gave speeches when he was not able.

After Dr. King was assassinated in Memphis, Tennessee in 1968, Coretta did not allow his dream to die with him. She continued Dr. King's fight for social justice and dedicated her life to his legacy. Her dedication and commitment led to the establishment of the Martin Luther King, Jr. Center for Nonviolent Social Change in Atlanta. Coretta actively fought for justice until her death in 2006. She will always be remembered as a great Civil Rights pioneer.

Maya Angelou, born in 1928, possesses a gift that enables her to both educate and inspire the multitudes. Angelou is a highly acclaimed poet and historian who endured a harsh childhood and early adulthood to achieve international status as a singer, actress, activist and writer. Her accomplishments include being nominated for a Pulitzer prize for the film Georgia, Georgia; serving on the American Revolution Bicentennial Commission, and on the Presidential Commission for International Year of the Woman; and reciting her poem "On the Pulse of the Morning" at President Clinton's inauguration in 1993.

Carol Moseley Braun, born in 1947, was the first and only Black woman elected to the United States Senate. In addition to this milestone, she was also the first Black senator to be elected as a Democrat and ran a brief campaign for the Democratic Party nomination in the 2004 U.S. presidential election.

Braun's accomplishments laid the foundation for many Blacks to excel in the political arena. As a successful politician and lawyer, she won many campaigns and received over 300 awards for achievements in the public interest. Currently, she is running a private law firm, Moseley Braun, LLC in Chicago.

Oprah Winfrey, born in 1954, was predetermined to achieve greatness and she did not allow an abusive childhood to rob her of her God-given talent. She rose above the madness and excelled. A force to be reckoned with, Oprah started her broadcasting career while still in high school and at age 19, became the first Black woman to anchor the news at Nashville's WTVF-TV. Capitalizing on her gift, Oprah relocated to Baltimore, Maryland where she worked for Baltimore's WJZ-TV as a news co-anchor. Driven and skilled, Oprah also co-hosted the local talk show, People are Talking.

In 1984, she journeyed to Chicago to host a morning talk show and within one month of her arrival, the show outshone its competition and was ranked number one. Due to Oprah's greatness, the show expanded to one hour and was renamed after her. And in 1986 The Oprah Winfrey Show entered national syndication while also earning the highest ratings in television history. Two years later, Oprah established Harpo Studios, making her the third woman in the U.S. entertainment industry to own her own studio. Through hard work and persistence she became the first Black woman to reach billionaire status.

Oprah is respected internationally as a talk show host, actress, philanthropist and entertainment mogul. She gives wholeheartedly and is responsible for positively influencing and improving the lives of millions.

Condoleezza Rice, born in 1954 currently serves as the National Security Advisor to President George W. Bush. She currently leads the White House's largest policy staff. Rice is the first Black woman to hold this position and earned it by excelling in several powerful positions in both the academic and political arenas. Rice is one of the most powerful Black women in the United States and takes pride in doing excellent work.

Take a moment to think about what you just read and your life overall. Do you believe that you are capable of accomplishing what your heart desires? The women who came before you proved that you are destined to achieve greatness and the world is yours to conquer. I believe in you. I also believe you are a Queen who deserves only the best. Again, I ask, "Do you consider yourself to be a Queen?" Your perception of your worth influences what you expect and value. What do you expect? What do you value? Are your expectations rational? Are your values consistent with your expectations? In the next chapter, we will explore your expectations and values.

Questions for Reflection and Discussion

Do you consider yourself to be a Queen? Yes or No (Explain)

Do you believe that you are the best or most important of your kind? Yes or No

Do you represent an abstract quality —A quality that is difficult to describe? Is it unique to you?

Are you the personification of optimism?

Are you a woman who embodies hope? Yes or No

Do you possess traits Queens exemplify: supreme and self-governing? Yes or No (Explain)

Do you respect yourself? Yes or No (Explain)

48

Have you gained the respect of others? Yes or No (Explain)

Use the space below to record your feelings and/or thoughts about this chapter. What did you learn?

*Notes*_____

_____
_____
_____
_____
_____
_____
_____
_____
_____
_____
_____
_____
_____
_____
_____
_____
_____
_____
_____
_____
_____
_____
_____
_____
_____
_____

One had better die fighting against injustice than die like a dog or a rat in a trap.

—Ida Wells-Barnett

Explore Your Expectations and Values

----------- *Chapter 4* -----------

Do you expect people to know what you need? Do you expect life to be fair all the time? Do you expect to be strong and perfect all the time? Do you expect to be treated fairly all the time? Do you expect to go through life without being hurt? If you answered *yes* to any question, you need to explore your expectations? Exploring your expectations is critical to preventing burnout and demoralization.

Explore your expectations or beliefs frequently and strive for excellence. A woman who believes that she is a Queen will expect others to treat her like one. Learn to stand-up for yourself and stop living with fear in your heart and mind. Fear is a reality of life and can be conquered. "For God hath not given us the spirit of fear; but of power, and of love, and of a sound mind" (2 Timothy 1:7). Some of you have been hurt one too many times and now you expect that every man or person who comes into your life will hurt you. You guard yourself by putting on your emotional armor. However, you allow men to enter your life and easily deceive you because you are vulnerable and hurt from previous failed relationships. You realize that they are being deceptive, but allow the behavior because you are hurt, angry or feel hopeless. These emotions handicap you. You feel vulnerable and hopeless so you do not expect much and are willing to accept whatever you can get. Some of you allow men to have sex with you, come and go as they please, spend the majority of their time hanging out with the boys, watching TV or playing games. You do not hold them accountable or demand that they respect you. You desire to be respected, but do not respect yourself. **I remind you that respect starts with self and is exemplified through action!**

The expectations you have of yourself, others and life in general often reflect how you live your life. Your expectations influence how you treat others and how you expect others to treat you. They also influence your view of yourself and others. Learn to replace irrational expectations with rational expectations.

Irrational expectations often develop from misperceptions or as a result of rigid and absolutist thinking. Let's look at some examples of both.

Misperceptions: Not accurate

"I can't expect him to do anything. He is not going to change. He is just like other men."

While there are similarities among men, each man is unique. Generalizing or categorizing does not allow you to view situations objectively. In addition, this particular expectation causes you to expect less. If you expect less, then you will probably accept less, which will likely result in you doing more, thus reinforcing your irrational expectation.

"Those who really care about me will know I'm feeling overwhelmed."

What's irrational about this expectation? You expect people to read your mind instead of telling them how you feel. If you tell them how you feel they can probably help you look at your problems more objectively.

"He will not leave me if I go out of my way to please him."

To be truthful you can do everything in your power and still be abandoned or rejected. You are less likely to be rejected if you present your true self in the beginning. He can take or leave it.

"I can do it all by myself."

Unfortunately many of you are doing it by yourself, but at what cost? Are you burning out? Do you feel overwhelmed? Are you happy? Are you undermining your values? The stress of taking care of others and yourself can be over-whelming.

There is pressure to do it all by yourself: take care of children, husband or boyfriend while maintaining a career and home. While many feel a sense of accomplishment, others feel guilt when they are too tired to perform all the tasks. Without help you will find yourself falling further into frustration and despair. You can't expect to do it all and stay emotionally and physically healthy. Teach others to respect your needs by setting limits. Do not allow others to cause you to burn out.

Rigid and Absolutist thinking: Some of you use rigid and absolute words such as should and must when describing your expectations. When you express "should and must" statements toward others, you feel guilt, anger, frustration and resentment when things do not work out.

"He *must* love me if I love him."

This is not rational. This absolutist thinking can cause you to feel rejected, angry and sad if your love is not returned. Life offers no guarantees. Replace this irrational expectation with, "It would be nice if he returned my love." Remember you are choosing to share your love. This approach empowers you and gives you control over your emotions.

"If I show respect I *should* get it back."

What is wrong with this statement? It confuses desire with obligation. It also reflects an idea of entitlement. Just because you desire something does not mean others should be obligated to do it. Try this: "If I show respect I prefer to be treated the same."

"I *must* be strong always."

The word "must" means that it has to happen and the word "always" does not allow a break. What's the worst that can happen if you are not strong? You might get hurt. Being hurt is part of life and those who live life to the fullest will get hurt. Unfortunately, people hurt each other. Learn to understand, embrace and grow from your pain and do not allow it to handicap you.

You are unique and gifted, but you are not capable of being strong always. Like everyone else, you need a break and due to different life circumstances you will occasionally be forced to take one even when you do not want it. If you allow yourself to function with irrational expectations for prolonged periods of time you will eventually burn out.

"If I am kind and/or nice to people, I *should* be treated the same."

This statement includes the idea of fairness. The decision to be nice is a personal choice. How people respond to you is their personal choice. Do what you feel comfortable doing and take responsibility for your emotions and actions. What's fair to one person is not fair to another. You can't control another individual unless they allow it.

"Do it right or not at all."

The results of expecting that you must behave perfectly can lead to lowered self-esteem and discouragement if you fail to do it right. This irrational thinking does not allow for mistakes, which facilitate growth. Individuals learn from practicing.

As a Queen you should have high expectations, but not irrational ones. If you desire to be in a relationship, you should make an effort to be with a man who is striving mentally, spiritually and financially. Do not settle for a man who cannot stimulate you mentally through intelligent conversation, uplift you spiritually by faith and support you financially by maintaining a job. Bond with a man who is sensitive enough or interested in understanding what you go through as a woman and will strive to keep you grounded. You need a man you can respect. And I encourage you to be submissive, but only if you respect him. Do not submit to a man who does not take care of his business; stop wasting your time. Give yourself to a God-fearing man who is worthy of having you and will honor God and you by making you his wife. "Marriage is honorable in all, and the bed undefiled: but whoremongers and adulterers God will judge" (Hebrews 13:4). As previously stated, God created man and woman to complete each other and live as one. He did not create you to be alone or to take care of a man. Expect a lot and you shall receive a lot because you are worthy of a lot.

If you desire to be in a relationship or be married, be patient and respect yourself. Do not chase any man. Allow your King to find you. A man who understands your worth and strives to comply with God's **Word**, will find and pursue you. God rewards all who abide by his **Word** and Proverbs 18:22 informs all men, especially Christian men that God will reward them for finding you: "He who finds a wife finds what is good and receives favor from the Lord."

Eliminate irrational and rigid expectations and replace them with rational and healthy expectations and I assure you that your life will be filled with meaningful and productive relationships. Now let's review your values.

Understanding what is most valuable to you helps guide your life. As children, we adopt values our parents and other adults possess. However, as we mature we learn to think for ourselves and begin to examine our past values. Based on our life experiences we decide to keep some values, reject others and develop new values to fit our current lifestyles and/or your expectations. The process of clarifying your values can help you gain a deeper understanding of yourself. Values often drive behavior. For example, a woman who values "helping" might spend a great deal of her time, money and energy helping others. While this value is noteworthy it can lead to burnout if she does not value **health** or engage in activities that address her emotional, physical and spiritual needs in a healthy manner. Certain values can affect others. Taking care of ourselves is paramount if we desire to sustain the ability to help others.

Individuals regularly invest their time, energy and money into things they value. What do you value? Review the values listed below and explore how they influence your lifestyle.

- Helping

You are very aware of the needs of others and attempt to help. You have a desire to make the world a better place.

- Health

You strive to improve and/or maintain your emotional, physical and spiritual status.

- Success

You want to be well-known or famous. Being on top or achieving your goals is very important to you.

- Relationships

You like people. Your family and friends are most important. You actively seek relationships and enjoy being in them. You feel energized by them.

- Financial Stability

You might choose a good salary over job satisfaction or an abusive partner who is financially stable over a loving man who is not.

- Honesty

You feel it is very important to be trusted and always honest.

- Hard work

You feel it is very important to labor to get want you want.

- Material items (nice car, home, etc.)

You feel that it is important to have nice things.

Throughout my college experience I was exposed to knowledge that challenged me to reevaluate my value system. I learned that the values I held as a child reflected what was important at that time in my life. We often shift our values to meet life challenges. During the Jim Crow era many Blacks valued family, relationships, hard work and helping others. Black men valued Black women and treated them like Queens. Although times were rough, elderly Black people commonly refer to those days as the good ole days and express sadness and unhappiness with how Black women are treated and viewed today. Unfortunately, a significant percentage of today's Black women are no longer being referred to as Queens, but instead are being called Hood Rats, Freaks, Gold Diggers and Chicken Heads. We are living in times when Black women are perceived to be less nurturing, self-centered and selfish! *What happened?* Are today's Black women's values different from those of our ancestors? As a Black woman have you taken the time to examine your value system?

Through personal and professional conversations with hundreds of Black women, I learned that *today's* Black women embrace values similar to those of our ancestors, but have reprioritized them. Here's how Trina, a 34 year old single and successful business woman, listed her values, in order of importance, as compared to our ancestors.

Our Ancestors	*Trina*
1) Helping	1) Financial Stability
2) Relationships	2) Success
3) Hard work	3) Hard work
4) Honesty	4) Health
5) Health	5) Honesty
6) Success	6) Helping
7) Financial Stability	7) Relationships
8) Material items	8) Material items

Do you agree with Trina's list? Perhaps you have a different view from Trina and would rank your values differently. Again, our values and views are influenced by our personal experiences. Trina's list might not accurately reflect how you would prioritize your values, but various Black women with whom I conversed reported that their values are similar to Trina's. To better understand this value shift, I decided to talk with a number of elderly Black women in our community. Through stimulating discussions, I learned that the '60s marked the beginning of hopelessness for many Blacks, especially Black women. Prior to 1960, Blacks successfully held their families intact. The negative impact of slavery, reconstruction, the Jim Crow era and the migration North did not totally destroy the Black family system. However, Blacks' ability to maintain a healthy family system declined significantly as the economy shifted. Manufacturing jobs most commonly held by Black males declined, causing considerable stress for them. This unfortunate situation along with the growth of women's economic independence was the beginning of the breakdown of the family system. In addition, increased drug trafficking in Black communities and the war on drugs further contributed to the collapse of the family system, as large numbers of Black males were imprisoned nationwide. With the absence of Black males in homes and in the community, Black women were left to perform the dual responsibilities of nurturer and bread-winner. And as a result of this unfortunate phenomenon many Black women were forced to reprioritize their values.

Performing in this dual capacity was necessary for survival. Black women quickly learned to fend for themselves and their children. In addition to taking care of responsibilities at home, they entered the work force to gain a sense of financial stability. Working was a means to pay bills and take care of household responsibilities. **Survival took precedence over other issues.**

With increased hopelessness in the Black community, values shifted and Black women were viewed differently. In an attempt to cope with this harsh phenomenon, secure happiness and relieve negative feelings many Black women engaged in demoralizing behavior, such as partying, drug use and sex for money. The phrase, *"Shake what your mama gave you"* was popularized in the Black community in the '90s and unfortunately many Black women did just that. And instead of others trying to understand their plight, they judged, labeled and condemned Black women. Those who condemned were usually doing well in life; had nice jobs, homes and cars and could not understand how some Black women could engage in such demoralizing behavior. This unjust condemnation contributed to negative feelings experienced by many Black women, thus reinforcing the demoralizing behavior. I do not agree with the behavior, but now I understand it. Blaming Black women for this phenomenon is not the answer. Nevertheless, I do believe that many Black women need to explore their values in order to reclaim their crowns and also prevent further burnout and demoralization.

Do your economic and social challenges influence your values? Through self-exploration you can learn to clarify your values and reprioritize them to help you function productively and live according to God's commandments.

Rank your values from the most to least important:

1.	5.
2.	6.
3.	7.
4.	8.

It is a fatal mistake to live life without occasionally clarifying your values. Having a clear understanding of why you do what you do is essential to your growth. Do not continue to be victimized by this harsh phenomenon. I realize that our social system is not good and Brothers are not carrying their weight, but you can help yourself by modifying values that make you feel guilty, frustrated, bitter, fatigued or ashamed. I value you and ask you to value yourself. When you feel discouraged, pray and ask God for strength, but do not engage in demoralizing behavior. God can and will provide, but you must believe that you can do all things through Christ (Philippians 4:13).

Questions for Reflection and Discussion

Do you expect people to know what you need?
Yes or No (Explain)

Do you expect life to be fair all the time?
Yes or No (Explain)

Do you expect to be strong or perfect all the time?
Yes or No (Explain)

Do you expect to go through life without being hurt?
Yes or No (Explain)

Do your values cause hardships for you? Yes or No

Do you need to explore your values and reprioritize them?
Yes or No

Why is it important to explore you values?

Use the space below to record your feelings and/or thoughts about this chapter. What did you learn?

*Notes*_____

_____

_____

_____

_____

_____

_____

_____

_____

_____

_____

_____

_____

_____

_____

_____

_____

_____

_____

_____

_____

_____

_____

_____

_____

_____

_____

_____

_____

If you don't like something, change it. If you can't change it, change your attitude. Don't complain.

—*Maya Angelou*

Change Your Attitude

----------- *Chapter 5* -----------

Some of you have been hurt and some of you are afraid of being hurt so you develop an attitude to protect yourself. It is only natural to distrust others when they hurt you, lie to you, betray you, and cause or contribute to your pain or frustration. However, many of you allow the fear of being hurt to consume you. You live your life being suspicious of others. Your attitude is defensive and you protect yourself and your love ones. This armor prevents you from feeling insecure or vulnerable. You feel safe functioning in this capacity, but do not realize that your pain and frustration results from your attitude. Among these attitudes are:

- I don't need a man. I am a strong Black woman.
- I don't care anymore.
- I will not be hurt ever or again.
- I have to get mine no matter what it takes.
- I don't have time. I am too busy.

Step back for a moment and check your attitude. Does one of the attitudes listed above register on your attitude meter? Many of you suffer because you do not check your attitude frequently or at all.

How you live your life reflects your attitude about life and often shapes how others view you. Some individuals might view you as being harsh and intolerable, while others might view you as a strong and independent woman. Nevertheless, a frequent check can be healthy.

While it is normal to protect yourself from being hurt, I do not believe that it is healthy to maintain self-defeating attitudes that can potentially lead to burnout and demoralization. By now you might be asking, "What does my attitude have to do with burnout or demoralization?" I am glad you asked.

Certain attitudes can lead to distrust and coldness. Distrusting others often makes you feel like you have to do it yourself, which can lead to burnout. Coldness can cause you to have little respect for yourself and/or others, which can lead to demoralization. You might find yourself frequently questioning others' intentions and behavior without valid reason. You might unconsciously distance yourself emotionally and overreact to small challenges. You might enter into a relationship or engage in sex, but detach emotionally to prevent yourself from being hurt. You might stay in a relationship that is not healthy for you. You might engage in activities that undermine your values (having sex for money, selling or using drugs, etc.). Over time you become sufficiently bitter and cold; people start avoiding you or treating you how you treat them. Unless you check and change your attitude, this process can become a troublesome, self-defeating approach. Here are five examples:

Case Illustration #1: Rose's Story

Rose was a 34-year-old Black female college graduate and successful partner in a large law firm, divorced, with no children. She was seeking treatment because she was having trouble coping with her failed marriage and dating. Here's her story:

I guess I was pretty bitter and angry after my husband left. During our marriage I did everything a woman should or could do. I cooked, cleaned and took care of his needs while working. I made love to him even when I was tired. Whatever he wanted I tried my best to give it.

We did not have any noticeable problems and I assumed we were happily married. However, about 5 years into our marriage he began to distance himself. He did not spend much time with me or want to be intimate. When I asked him what was going on he told me that he was falling out of love with me. I was totally surprised and pleaded with him to stay. I asked if we could seek marital therapy and he said no.

My husband was very stubborn and often did not share his emotions. If we had a disagreement he would withdraw. After a while I figured out that I would be better off if I did not pursue him. Unfortunately, he left me.

To this day I do not know why he left, but I eventually moved on with my life. I swore that I would never be hurt again. **I date occasionally, but I do not take men seriously.** I built myself back up. I am a strong Black woman. I really don't need a man. I can take care of myself financially. I meet nice guys, but I often chase them away after a few dates. I don't express emotions frequently or let them know that I am enjoying them. They tell me that I have an "**I don't care attitude**." I don't see anything wrong with me. Someday I would like to get married again, but I struggle. What do I need to do?

Case Illustration #2: Pam's Story

Pam was a 25-year-old Black female high school graduate, manager of a fast food restaurant, single, with three children. She was seeking treatment because she was suffering from low self-esteem and having trouble finding a good man that will love and respect her. Here's her story:

During my childhood, I was physically and sexually abused. When I was twelve years old, my mother left me with one of her male friends who molested me. This happened several more times and I never told anyone for years.

For years I believed that I was worthless and struggled to love any man. I dated guys who always wanted sex. I never thought anything was wrong with it because I like sex. Unfortunately, none of my children have the same father. The men usually leave me after I get pregnant. I tried to do right by being with one man, but it did not work out. **I don't try to do the right thing anymore.** Doing the right thing does not get my children fed or pay my bills so I use my body to get money. I have to get mine no matter what it takes. Caring got me three children and no man. If a man wants to be with me he has to accept me the way I am. I am a survivor and I let men know upfront. I really want to be loved and I know I should not do some of the things I do, but *I don't care anymore.* What do I need to do?

Case Illustration #3: Tina's Story

Tina was a 28-year-old Black female high school graduate, stay-home wife, with two children. She was seeking treatment because she was suffering from burnout that began one year ago. Here's her story:

During my childhood I had to take care of myself and my siblings. I could not rely on my parents because they were drug addicts. I cooked, cleaned and did what was needed to maintain our household. I grew up believing that I could not trust people. I learned to take care of things by myself.

I married early. Shortly after I married I felt that it was o.k. to ask my husband to help me. He helped whenever I asked and sometimes when I did not, but for some reason I felt like he would eventually let me down, so I stopped

70

asking for help. **I look for the worst in situations and
sometimes my attitude can be negative.** I practically
cooked, cleaned and raised our children by myself. If I
wanted things done, I did it myself. I realize that I need to
share my feelings, but I don't have time. I am too busy.

I don't want to feel this way. What do I need to do?

Case Illustration #4: Gina's Story

Gina was a 19 year-old Black female college student, with
no children. She was seeking treatment because she was
suffering from low self-esteem. Here's her story:

As a young girl I grew up watching all the popular girls get
what they want by having sex with boys. I never understood
them, but wanted to be like them because they appeared to
be happy. Everyone liked them and wanted to be around
them. So after I entered college I approached one of the
popular girls on campus and asked how I could be popular
and get what I want from guys. She said to have sex with
them. She told me that if I wanted to be popular I would do
whatever it takes. I started engaging in the same behavior
and developed an **"It's all about me, I don't care" attitude**.
I was very popular, but I did not like what I was doing.
Others saw me as this confident, outgoing young lady, but
on the inside I was not confident. My new attitude got me
attention, but the wrong kind of attention.
I don't want to feel this way. What do I need to do?

Case Illustration #5: Lisa's Story

Lisa was a 25-year-old Black female high school graduate,
with no children. She was seeking treatment because she
was having a hard time bonding with men. Here's her story:

I don't know where to begin. I just do not trust men. My father left when I was 12 after he abused my mother for years and my two brothers are dogs. I want to be in a relationship, but I am afraid of being hurt. I have tried a few times, but things did not go well. In anticipation that I would get hurt, I usually did something to test them. I would make them upset to see what they would do. I know I play games, but I don't want to get hurt first. **"Sometimes I care and sometimes I do not."** I have casual relationships, but find ways to end them before they get too serious. Life is about protecting yourself because no one else will. I don't want to be hurt, but I do want to fall in love someday.

I don't want to feel this way. What do I need to do?

Change Your Attitude

Unfortunately, many of you go through life with negative and/or self-defeating attitudes. Through various personal life experiences or observation of others' experiences you develop attitudes. If your life experiences have been positive or you have high self-esteem you are likely to exhibit positive attitudes. On the other hand, if your life experiences have been negative or you have low self-esteem you are likely to exhibit negative attitudes.

Women and young girls who go through life with negative, self-defeating attitudes are at greater risk for burnout and demoralization. Learn to replace negative/self-defeating attitudes with positive attitudes:

Negative/Self-defeating Attitudes:

- I don't need a man. I am a strong Black woman.
- I don't care anymore.
- I will not be hurt ever or again.
- I have to get mine no matter what it takes.

- I don't need anybody.
- I don't have time. I am too busy.

Positive Attitudes:

- I don't need a man to survive, but God created man and woman to be of one. I can have a man and still be a strong Black woman.
- Caring for others is healthy. Unfortunately, I might not always get it back. I choose to care for others and accept the risk. Bitterness is destructive.
- Unfortunately, pain and suffering are part of life. I cannot always avoid them, but I can learn to cope with them effectively.
- I can get my needs met in healthy and productive ways.
- The need to belong is important. Family and friends can be a source of support.
- Managing my time can reduce my stress and encourage positive emotions.

Changing your attitude is achievable and can give you control over your life. But to successfully change your attitude you must be honest with yourself and admit that you need to change. Apply the 9 strategies below to see how you can replace negative, self-defeating attitudes that may have prevented you from being happy in the past.

1.)   **Identify a negative or self-defeating attitude** you have about something in your life and write it down here. It may be educational, personal or social. Identifying a specific attitude will encourage you to do something. Write it here.

_____

_____

_____

_____

_____

_____

2.)   **Affirm to yourself that you intend to change** and write down a statement that reflects your intention to change the negative or self-defeating attitude above. Also rephrase the negative or self-defeating statement into a positive statement. Write it here.

_____

_____

_____

_____

_____

_____

3.)   **Identify two people who you believe possess the positive attitude you desire to have** and list how they express this attitude. This step encourages you to model your behavior after someone you admire or respect.

_____

_____

_____

_____

_____

_____

74

4.)   Identify three different behaviors you can do that demonstrate to others you have a new attitude. Practice makes perfect and reinforces your desired attitude.

_____

_____

_____

_____

_____

_____

5.)   Explain three situations in which you frequently find yourself where you could practice the three behaviors listed above. Behavior that is conducted often results in a habit.

_____

_____

_____

_____

_____

_____

6.)   Identify three people you can talk to about changing your attitude and ask them to support you and hold you accountable. Most of us try to stand by our words and do well with support.

_____

_____

_____

_____

_____

_____

7.) **Identify three times during the day when you intend to imagine what you will be like and how you will feel** once you acquire this new attitude and apply it. Visual images help some of us perform.

_____

_____

_____

_____

_____

_____

8.) **Write down at least one thing you will do for yourself as a reward for developing** a new positive attitude. Rewarding ourselves often encourages us to repeat behaviors or patterns of thinking.

_____

_____

_____

_____

_____

_____

9.) **Identity two individuals you can teach this approach to.** Giving back is fundamental and encourages growth in yourself and others.

_____

_____

_____

_____

_____

_____

76

Life will bring challenges and your attitude will determine how you cope with and address them. Changing your attitude is not the sole solution to solving your problems, but it is a solution that empowers you to control your emotions and life in general. We cannot always change our situations, but we can change our attitude. **You have more power than you know!**

Questions for Reflection and Discussion

Do you have a self-defeating or negative attitude?
Yes or No. If yes, Why? (Explain)

How does a negative attitude prevent you from having a happy life?

Can a negative or self-defeating attitude cause you to suffer from burnout and/or demoralization?

What can you do to establish a positive attitude?

Why is it important to maintain a positive attitude?

Who controls how you think and feel?

78

Use the space below to record your feelings and/or thoughts about this chapter. What did you learn?

*Notes*_____

_____
_____
_____
_____
_____
_____
_____
_____
_____
_____
_____
_____
_____
_____
_____
_____
_____
_____
_____
_____
_____
_____
_____
_____
_____
_____
_____
_____
_____

It doesn't matter who you are, where you come from. The ability to triumph begins with you. Always.

—*Oprah Winfrey*

Love Yourself Unconditionally

----------- *Chapter 6* -----------

The ability to love yourself unconditionally can be challenging, especially if you have experienced hardships such as sexual, physical or emotional abuse. However, remember that your life experiences do not define who you are. Unfortunately, bad things happen to good people. Your ability to cope with hardships defines your true character. Do not fall victim to loving yourself based on conditions. Love yourself regardless of your appearance, background or economic, social or financial status. I realize that this is a difficult task because people can be very judgmental, but remember that God did not create perfect people. We all have fallen short of his glory. Some individuals may appear to have it all together. They might appear to be perfect, but Jesus was the only perfect human that walked this earth. Do not live your life stressing about being perfect. Instead live it doing the best you can. Challenge yourself to objectively and effectively eliminate emotions, expectations and attitudes that make you feel unlovable.

You are special because you share in the image of God. When you are feeling down remember that life is a gift from God. Need I say more? Your ability to love yourself unconditionally depends on what you tell yourself, how you treat yourself, and how you interpret your world. If loving yourself requires others to approve of you, you might find yourself feeling frustrated, helpless and powerless. Seeking the approval of others can lead to burnout and demoralizing behavior. Work at loving yourself and improving your self-esteem. People with high self-esteem view themselves positively. They often feel good about themselves and understand their worth.

Now that I have your undivided attention and you are inspired to love yourself unconditionally let's look at six self-empowering strategies you can implement to improve your self-esteem, which will optimistically help you learn to love yourself unconditionally.

1. Love God First
2. Set your own personal standards
3. Use encouraging, positive language
4. Identify your strengths
5. Eliminate self-defeating/irrational thinking
6. Do away with perfectionist thinking

Strategy 1: Love God First. God created us to love him, but many of us look for love in all the wrong places. True happiness and unconditional love for yourself or others will not occur until you learn to love God first. God is love and He loves you unconditionally. You are His child. Do not distance yourself from your Father when "Evil" things happen to you or your love ones. Remember that God gave the gift of "Free Will." Be mindful that your attempt to walk righteously does not exclude you from experiencing bad things. Others have "Free Will" as well and when they choose to love and be of the World instead of God, Evil things will happen. Evil is present where God is absent. Keep God in your heart, mind and soul and loving yourself unconditionally will come with effortlessness. Your unconditional love for self and others is only possible by reordering your love, God first.

Therefore if any man be in Christ, he is a new creature: old things are passed away; behold, all things are become new (II Corinthians 5:17).

But seek ye first the kingdom of God, and his righteousness; and all these things shall be added unto you (Matthew 6:33)

Strategy 2: Set your own personal standards. To start loving yourself, simply set your own standards. Do not live your life according to how others view you. Avoid comparing yourself to others and using belittling words such as stupid, ugly, worthless, fat, dumb, and shallow to describe you. Pay close attention to how you define and/describe yourself and remove negative self-attacks.

Strategy 3: Use encouraging, positive language. "The tongue of the wise useth knowledge aright: but the mouth of fools poureth out foolishness" (Proverbs 15:2). When you talk to yourself and to others about yourself use positive and inspiring statements. Such statements are called affirmations. Effective use of affirmations can help you change problem areas in your life. Identify a problem in your life and set a gratifying goal. Some examples of affirmations include:

- I am a queen and worthy of being treated like one.
- I dress well and really feel good about it.
- I can take care of myself in a healthy manner.
- I handle disappointment calmly and reasonably.
- I have a right to make mistakes.
- I can let go of my need to control others.
- I cope with despair and pain rationally.

Learn to write affirmations that use present tense, define what you want, what already exists, and what makes you feel good. Use specific, personal, action-oriented words that are short and to the point. Develop a list of affirmations that are meaningful to you and practice them daily. If your affirmations do not produce your desired outcome, write new ones. Remember that what you say to yourself and others is often stored subconsciously in your mind and theirs.

Strategy 4: Identify your strengths. Conduct an accurate and truthful self-assessment and develop a valid list of your strengths and assets. If you suffer from low self-esteem it probably did not occur over night. Remind yourself of your strengths daily and take an inventory. Use your inventory to help you identify blessings, accomplishments and goals you have established that support your dreams and ambitions.

Strategy 5: Eliminate self-defeating/irrational beliefs. Question your old beliefs and replace them with new ones. Too often many of you hold on to unhealthy beliefs with which you grew up. Some of your beliefs are healthy and some are not. If the following beliefs are in your mind eliminate them:

-If I ask for help, I'll look weak.
-If people knew the real me, they would dislike me.
-If I fail, I'm a loser.
-I should never feel powerless, tired or depressed.
-I am nothing unless I am loved.
-I should be totally self-sufficient and independent.
-I have to be right all the time or I won't be respected.
-I am the only one who understands me and can solve my problems.
-If I try hard enough, I can succeed at anything and everything
-Some people are better than others.

-I need to be smart, rich, powerful and attractive to be happy.
-Life isn't fair, and I can't handle it.
-It reflects poorly on me if my relationship or marriage does not work.

Eliminating self-defeating/irrational thinking can help you see and experience life more objectively. Your mind is powerful and if used inappropriately it can cause you to self-destruct. Examine your beliefs and ask yourself several questions. What evidence do I have to support my beliefs? Are my beliefs beneficial or healthy? Do they make me feel good or bad? After carefully reviewing your beliefs you might find that you need to eliminate some of them and replace them with new ones. Don't be discouraged or beat yourself during this process. Changing your way of thinking can be a complex process. After all, you did not become the person you are overnight.

Strategy 6: Do away with perfectionist thinking. While it is important to look, feel and do well, remember that you are not and will never be perfect. Striving for perfection can lead to unrealistic expectations of yourself and others. Do your best and accept yourself while enhancing your performance and having fun. Life is too short to live it thinking you must do everything perfectly or not at all. Perfectionist thinking can lead to hard work and no play. You cannot do it all. Enjoy life, yourself and others and ask for help when you need it.

Improving your self-esteem and loving yourself unconditionally can be one of the most rewarding things you will ever do. Do not let others rob you of your gift of life. God created you out of love so you can love yourself and others. Don't be afraid to love yourself. The benefits can be profound. Nelson Mandela glorified the importance of loving yourself and living without fear by stating, "And as we let our light shine, we unconsciously give other people permission to do the same. As we're liberated from our own fear, our presence automatically liberates others."

What Now?

To love yourself unconditionally, practice the strategies listed above daily, share your commitment with others and use the following quotations for inspiration:

"I believe that unarmed truth and unconditional love will have the final word in reality. This is why right, temporarily defeated, is stronger than evil triumphant."
—Martin Luther King, Jr.

"The ultimate lesson all of us have to learn is unconditional love, which includes not only others but ourselves as well."
—Elisabeth Kubler-Ross

"Apply Strategies"

Identify a problem or issue you are experiencing that negatively influences how you view yourself and apply the strategies to improve your self-esteem and increase your ability to love yourself unconditionally.

Strategy 1: Love God first

_____
_____
_____
_____
_____
_____
_____

Strategy 2: Set your own personal standards

_____
_____
_____
_____
_____
_____
_____

Strategy 3: Use encouraging, positive language

_____
_____
_____
_____
_____
_____
_____

88

Strategy 4: Identify Your Strengths

_____

_____

_____

_____

_____

_____

Strategy 5: Eliminate self-defeating/irrational beliefs

_____

_____

_____

_____

_____

_____

Strategy 6: Do away with perfectionist thinking

_____

_____

_____

_____

_____

_____

Questions for Reflection and Discussion

Do you love yourself unconditionally? Yes or No (Explain)

Do you love others unconditionally? Yes or No (Explain)

Why should you love yourself and others unconditionally?

Is God's love unconditional? Yes or No

What did God do to demonstrate his unconditional love for us? (Explain)

What are you going to do to start loving yourself?

Use the space below to record your feelings and/or thoughts about this chapter. What did you learn?

*Notes*_____

_____
_____
_____
_____
_____
_____
_____
_____
_____
_____
_____
_____
_____
_____
_____
_____
_____
_____
_____
_____
_____
_____
_____
_____
_____
_____
_____
_____
_____
_____

Change is a personal phenomenon— Our dilemma is that we hate change and love it at the same time; what we want is for things to remain the same but get better.

-Sydney Harris

Conclusion

As you have read through this book I hope it enhanced your understanding of your worth and equipped you with tools to prevent burnout and/or demoralization. I also hope that you realize that you are a Queen and the backbone of the Black community. Your worth is not defined by your physical or emotional traits, economic or financial status, accomplishments or success, but by your God-given attributes. God has blessed you to be capable of healing the sick and comforting the distressed, but he also wants you to respect and take care of yourself. Do not allow bad relationships, limited household resources or poor environmental conditions cause you to diminish your God-given gift. Keep it "R.E.A.L.". You cannot expect God to protect you from every bad thing in this world, but you can rest assure that he loves you. After all, you are a Queen!

Think like a queen. A queen is not afraid to fail. Failure is another steppingstone to greatness.

—Oprah Winfrey

Appendix 1

A Black Woman's Creed!

I am responsible for how I am treated.

My expectations of myself will influence how others treat me.

It is my duty to respect myself and demand it from others.

What I see in the mirror is what I get and I attract who I am.

I will make an effort to correct character flaws when identified and accept constructive feedback without attitude.

I realize that I am not perfect, but I am worthy of being treated like a Queen!

Respect starts with self and is exemplified through action!

Dwayne L. Buckingham

Appendix 2

A Black Man's Creed!
My Queen and Backbone!

I am responsible for how I treat Black women.

A real man does not take advantage of a woman or anyone else.

I will model behavior that I would expect my son to model.

I will approach and treat every Black woman with respect, dignity and sincerity regardless of how she presents herself.

I will express my gratitude frequently and with words.

I cannot expect a Black woman to treat me like a King if I am not willing to treat her like the Queen she is!

Love comes from the heart, not the mind! I get what I give!

Dwayne L. Buckingham

--------------------A Black Woman's Worth!--------------------

Appendix 3

One Flaw in Women

Women have strengths that amaze men.
They bear hardships and carry burdens,
but they hold happiness, love and joy.

They smile when they want to scream.
They sing when they want to cry.
They cry when they are happy,
and laugh when they are nervous.

They fight for what they believe in.
They stand up for injustice.
They don't take **no** for an answer
when they believe there is a better answer.
They go without so their family can have.
They go to the doctor with a frightened friend.
They love unconditionally.

They cry when their children excel
and cheer when their friends get an award.
They are happy when they hear about
a wedding or a birth.

Their heart breaks when a friend dies.
They grieve at the loss of a family member,
Yet they are strong when they
think there is no strength left.
They know that a hug and kiss
can heal a broken heart.

----------------------A Black Woman's Worth!----------------------

Women come in all sizes, shapes and colors.
They'll drive, run, walk or email you
to show how much they care about you.

The heart of a woman is what makes
the world keep turning.
They bring hope, joy and love.
They have compassion and ideas.
They give moral support to
their friends and family.
Women have vital things to say
and things to give.

However if there is one flaw in women,
It's that they forget their worth.
(Author unknown)

Appendix 4

100 MOST FASCINATING BLACK WOMEN OF THE 20th CENTURY
Ebony March 1999

THEY are, in the Nat Cole and Dinah Washington sense of the word, unforgettable. By a unique power, by unusual stature or the capture of a new beachhead for the Black or Black feminine or feminine personality, they attracted and held national attention, delighting us and challenging us and making us bigger: We can argue about this or that point or this or that person, but it is beyond question that these 100 are among the Black women without whom the century and the Black or American personality would be diminished.

OPRAH WINFREY

Actress, producer and indisputable queen of daytime television, she transformed the talk-show format and in the process became an international icon. As the producer-owner of her own show and the producer of several made-for-TV and theatrical releases, she is a major cultural force and one of the most powerful women in the entertainment industry.

MARY McLEOD BETHUNE (1875–1955)

Educator, founder of Bethune–Cookman College and the National Council of Negro Women, she was the first Black woman to receive a major U.S. government appointment and was the mentor and mother figure for generations of Black male and female leaders.

LENA HORNE

America's first real Black movie star, she paved the way for Black men and women in Hollywood. Her enduring and indelible career took her from cabaret performer in the '30s to stage and screen star in the '40s, '50s and '60s, and she's still recording today. She also was an early and active participant in the civil rights struggle, a foe of discrimination in the entertainment industry and the rest of America.

MADAME C. J. WALKER (1867-1919)

Enterprising hair-care entrepreneur, philanthropist and political activist, she developed the "hot-iron" process for straightening hair. Reputed to be the first self-made U.S. woman millionaire, she used her great wealth and business acumen to promote social and political change for Blacks and women.

MARGARET WALKER ALEXANDER (1915–1998)

Novelist, poet and educator, she is perhaps best known for her influential poem, For My People, which was published in 1942, and her critically acclaimed novel, Jubilee.

DEBBIE ALLEN

Actress, dancer, choreographer, director, producer, she is an amazingly versatile performer and entertainment industry executive. Whether navigating stormy Hollywood waters to produce Amistad or putting dancers through their paces as choreographer of the Academy Awards telecast, this multiple Emmy winner's boundless talents appear to be from a different world.

SADIE TANNER MOSSELL ALEXANDER (1898–1989)

Lawyer and civil rights activist, she was the first Black woman in the U.S. to receive a doctorate in economics. She was also one of the first Black women to obtain a law degree and practice law in Philadelphia. One of the founders of the National Bar Association she fought discrimination in Philadelphia hotels, restaurants and theaters.

MAYA ANGELOU

Poet, actress, icon, she electrified the nation with the poem she wrote for President Bill Clinton's 1992 inauguration. An immensely popular author (I Know Why The Caged Bird Sings) and social commentator, she made her debut as a director of feature films with the recently released Down in the Delta.

MARIAN ANDERSON (1902–1993)

Hailed as "a voice that comes along once in a generation," she was a major concert figure and a pioneer in classical music—the first Black singer signed by the Metropolitan Opera House. She made her Met debut in A Masked Ball in 1955.

JOSEPHINE BAKER (1906–1975)

International superstar, she was a magnetic singer-dancer who captivated Paris and the world. An outspoken foe of racism in the U.S. and a freedom fighter during the Nazi occupation of France, her adopted home, the St. Louis-born entertainer was cited for her heroism in World War II.

ELLA BAKER (1903–1986)

Brilliant organizer and activist, she helped to create the Southern Christian Leadership Conference and the Student Nonviolent Coordinating Committee.

IDA B. WELLS-BARNETT (1862–1931)

Editor, businesswoman, women's rights leader and a prolific and influential writer, she used her highly successful newspaper columns to spread the gospel of her anti-lynching crusade and promote equal rights.

ANGELA BASSETT

An incendiary screen presence, she is a classically trained actress and the embodiment of the beauty, intelligence and sensuality of the contemporary Black woman. In roles ranging from Betty Shabazz to Tina Turner, she displayed the wellspring of talent that has made her a Hollywood and audience favorite.

DAISY BATES & THE YOUNG WOMEN OF THE LITTLE ROCK 9

Bates, a newspaper editor and president of the Arkansas NAACP, was one of the major forces behind the Little Rock, Ark., school integration crisis of 1957. Six of the nine Little Rock teenagers who broke the race barrier at Central High School were young women: Thelma Mothershed, Elizabeth Eckford, Gloria Ray, Melba Pattilo, Carlotta Walls and Minnie Brown. (Jefferson Thomas, Ernest Green and Terrance Roberts ... were their male counterparts.) Their heroism catapulted them into the national spotlight and cemented their places in history.

HALLE BERRY

Sultry screen star who has emerged as a major presence in Hollywood. Smart, sexy and fiercely independent, her numerous film incarnations have helped redefine the role of Black women in movies.

JANE M. BOLIN

The first Black woman judge in the United States, she was appointed to the Domestic Relations Court of the City of New York in 1939 by then-Mayor Fiorello LaGuardia. She was also the first Black woman to graduate from Yale University Law School.

GWENDOLYN BROOKS

In 1950, this Chicago-based writer became the first Black American to win a Pulitzer Prize. She was cited for her collection of poems, Annie Allen. She has also been a mentor and major influence to a generation of younger writers.

CHARLOTTE HAWKINS BROWN (1883–1961)

Founder of the Palmer Memorial Institute, a private secondary school in Sedalia, N.C., and an influential educator and activist throughout the first half of the 20th century. She also was a founding member of the National Council of Negro Women.

NANNIE HELEN BURROUGHS (1879–1961)

Religious leader, educator and political organizer, she was the founder of the National Training School for Women and Girls in Washington, D.C. Her passionate speech at the annual conference of the National Baptist Convention in 1900 led to the formation of the Woman's Convention Auxiliary to the NBC, one of the largest Black women's organizations in America.

DIAHANN CARROLL

Singer and actress whose poise, beauty and talent helped break many barriers. In 1968, she changed the face of television when she became the first Black woman to have her own weekly television series, Julia. She subsequently became the first Black woman to star in a nighttime soap opera when she joined the cast of Dynasty in 1984.

SHIRLEY CHISHOLM

A groundbreaking political leader and activist. Voters in the Bedford-Stuyvesant section of Brooklyn made her the first Black woman in Congress in 1968. In 1972, she became the first Black person to mount a serious campaign for president.

ELIZABETH CATLETT

Painter and sculptor, often called the dean of Black women artists. She has won numerous awards for her interpretations of the struggles and triumphs of African-Americans.

ALICE COACHMAN

She leaped into the history books at the Olympic Games in 1948 when she became the first Black woman to win an

Olympic gold medal. She placed first in the high jump competition.

JOHNNETTA BETSCH COLE

Educator and anthropologist, she was the first Black woman to assume the presidency of Spelman College, She took the helm of the prestigious women's school in 1987 and during her decade-long reign established new benchmarks for academic excellence and the successful stewardship of a Black institution of higher learning.

BESSIE COLEMAN (1893–1926)

The first Black woman to earn a pilot's license, she learned to fly from top aviators in France, where she earned her international pilot's license. She was killed at age 33 in a flying accident on April 30, 1926. The founder of Christ Universal Temple in Chicago, she has been a symbol and role model for generations of women ministers. She began her ministry in 1956 with a congregation of five. Today, her church has more than 12,000 members.

MARVA COLLINS

Influential educator and founder of the Marva Collins Preparatory School in Chicago, she helped redefine educational achievement in the late 20th century by demonstrating that Black youngsters are capable of mastering difficult academic disciplines.

ANGELA DAVIS

Activist and educator, she became a worldwide symbol of Black pride and Black protest during the '70s. Her extensive writings and speeches continue to captivate and inspire a new generation of leaders committed to social change.

RITA DOVE

In 1993, she became the first Black poet laureate of the United States. She won the Pulitzer Prize in 1985 for her book of poetry, Thomas and Beulah.

DOROTHY DANDRIDGE (1922-1965)

A major sex symbol in Hollywood, her performance in Carmen Jones earned her an Academy Award nomination for best actress. She was the first Black actress to achieve that distinction.

KATHERINE DUNHAM

Internationally renowned choreographer, dancer and ethnographer, she brought the unique rhythms of Africa and the Caribbean to the concert stage and laid the foundation for contemporary Black dancers.

JOYCELYN ELDERS

The first Black woman to serve as U.S. Surgeon General, the physician was appointed by President Bill Clinton in 1992 and served until 1994. She remains a staunch advocate and educator concerning U.S. health issues.

MARIAN WRIGHT EDELMAN

The founder and chair of the Children's Defense Fund, she is the major advocate for U.S. children of all races and was an active participant in the Freedom Movement.

106

MYRLIE EVERS-WILLIAMS

Activist and business executive, she was an integral part of a historic team and led the successful struggle to bring Medgar Evers' assassin to justice. She later became the third woman to chair the NAACP.

ELLA FITZGERALD (1917–1996)

A true jazz innovator, she helped redefine U.S. popular singing, adding virtuoso stylings to frothy, "Tin Pan Alley" tunes. She remained at the front ranks of the entertainment industry from the '40s through the '90s

CRYSTAL BIRD FAUSET (1893–1965)

The first Black woman elected to a state legislature. Voters in the 18th District of Philadelphia elected her to the Pennsylvania House of Representatives in 1938. While she only served one year—resigning to take a post with the Works Progress Administration—she remained dedicated to improving the quality of life for African Americans.

ARETHA FRANKLIN

She went from gospel-singing prodigy to the high priestess of R-E-S-P-E-C-T. Along the way, she opened the doors for Whitney Houston, Janet Jackson and the new legion of pop-R&B divas. One of President Clinton's favorite entertainers, she was presented with a 1994 Kennedy Center Honors Award for her contributions to the world of music.

ALTHEA GIBSON

Burst through the all-White barriers of the tennis establishment to become the first Black to win titles at the U.S. Tennis Association Championship (now known as the U.S. Open) and Wimbledon. She won titles in both events in 1957 and '58.

ANN FUDGE

As the president of Maxwell House Coffee, she opened a new era for Black women in big business. Her ascension signaled that a new ethos had entered the executive suite and that corporate America, while enriched as much by her presence as by her business acumen, would not be quite the same.

CHARLAYNE HUNTER-GAULT

In 1961, she made news as one of the first Black students to enter the University of Georgia in Athens. Today, she is one of the most prominent Black journalists in the world, covering the vast political and social changes occurring in South Africa.

PAM GRIER

Her bad and beautiful screen persona made her a national icon during the height of the blaxploitation film craze of the '70s. As the statuesque, take-no-prisoners heroine of films such as Coffy and Foxy Brown, she blew audiences (and bad guys) away, and demonstrated the indomitability of the Black woman.

MOTHER HALE (1905–1992)

As the founder of "Hale House," an institution that gives care and hope to drug-addicted and abused children, Clara McBride Hale inspired a nation to reach out to its youngest victims.

LORRAINE HANSBERRY (1930–1965)

The first Black woman playwright to have a work produced on Broadway (A Raisin in the Sun), Hansberry also was an uncompromising foe of racism and oppression. In addition to gathering support for the Student Nonviolent Coordinating Committee, she also was a vocal critic of the House Un-American Activities Committee.

FANNIE LOU HAMER (1917–1977)

One of the major figures of the Freedom Movement, this civil rights activist challenged the injustice of Southern voting laws and was a pivotal force in the Freedom Democratic Party.

PATRICIA ROBERTS HARRIS (1924–1985)

The first Black woman to serve in a United States president's cabinet, she was tapped by President Jimmy Carter to serve as secretary of Housing and Urban Development in 1977. In 1980, Carter appointed her secretary of the Department of Health Education and Welfare.

THE RT. REV. BARBARA HARRIS

The first woman bishop of the Episcopal Church, she was consecrated in the Massachusetts diocese in 1989 and became an international symbol of the struggle for gender equality in the church.

ANNA ARNOLD HEDGEMAN (1899–1990)

Activist, author and social worker, she served under FDR as executive director of a commission dedicated to ensuring fair employment practices. She was a major architect of the 1963 March on Washington and was instrumental in securing passage of the Civil Rights Bill of 1964–65.

ANITA HILL

Law professor, lecturer and author, she became the defining symbol of the sexual harassment movement and the catalyst for the 1992 electoral victories that helped redefine the role of women in politics and business.

DOROTHY HEIGHT

A protégée of Mary McLeod Bethune, she led the National Council of Negro Women from 1957–97 and was a major leader of the Freedom Movement.

ALEXIS HERMAN

As Secretary of Labor to President Clinton, she's stood in the firestorm of contentious disputes and brought new sensibilities and sensitivities to the role of the nation's chief labor negotiator.

BILLIE HOLIDAY (1915–1959)

One of the most influential jazz singers of all time and an immensely popular nightclub performer and recording star of the '30s, '40s and '50s, She was one of the greatest song stylists of any era. Her haunting voice breathed new life into every lyric.

WHITNEY HOUSTON

One of the brightest stars in pop music, she has become a multidimensional entertainment industry mogul-producer, acquiring and starring in her own movies and television specials. Her unbroken string of hit recordings set new marks for musical excellence.

ZORA NEALE HURSTON (1901?–1960)

Anthropologist, novelist and pioneer scholar of Negro folklore, she was a key figure in the Harlem Renaissance and one of the most widely published authors of the '30s and '40s.

MAHALIA JACKSON (1911–1972)

One of the United States' greatest gospel singers, she transcended her field and became a national treasure. She helped make gospel music an integral part of the U.S. inspirational songbook and, in the process, gained fame well beyond the shores of the United States.

JANET JACKSON

She broke through musical and family barriers and shot to the top of the pop world, creating a new, multihued rhythm nation and announced that "Miss Jackson" is not just Michael's little sister, but a cultural force in her own right.

JUDITH JAMISON

The muse of legendary choreographer Alvin Ailey, she helped redefine modern dance and imbued the art form with a new vocabulary and spirituality culled from the African American experience. As the director of the Ailey dance company, she keeps her late mentor's work and vision alive.

MAE C. JEMISON

As a member of the seven-member crew aboard the space shuttle Endeavor, this physician became the first Black woman to travel into outer space. Her historic mission began on Sept. 12, 1992.

ELAINE JONES

As the first woman to head the NAACP Legal Defense and Education Fund, she not only tends the torch passed down from Thurgood Marshall, she has expanded the agency's scope to include tackling environmental issues as well as institutional racism.

HAZEL JOHNSON

The first Black woman general in the history of the U.S. military, she was appointed a brigadier general in the U.S. Army on Sept. 1, 1979, and served until her retirement in 1983.

FLORENCE GRIFFITH JOYNER (1959–1998)

A combination of grace, beauty and blazing speed, she dashed into the track and field record books in 1988 with gold medal-winning performances in the 100- and 200-meter events and the 400-meter relay at the XXIV Olympiad in Seoul.

BARBARA JORDAN (1936–1996)

One of the U.S.'s most admired women, she was the first Black Southern congresswoman, and she gained wide acclaim for her impassioned speeches during the Nixon impeachment hearings in 1974. One of the great orators of the 20th century and the first Black to give a keynote address at a major party convention, she electrified delegates at the Democratic convention of 1976.

THE REV. BARBARA KING

Founder and pastor of the Hillside Chapel and Truth Center in Atlanta, this dynamic minister and author (she has six books to her credit) leads a flock of 5,000 who are drawn to her ecumenical ministry and bold, uplifting preaching.

JACKIE JOYNER-KERSEE

Called the world's greatest female athlete, she was the first woman to win back-to-back gold medals in the Olympic heptathlon competition in the 1988 and 1992 Games.

THE REV. BERNICE KING

Ordained minister, attorney and public speaker, her passionate oratory—reminiscent of her late father—is reinterpreting and reinforcing the dream for a new generation of dreamers.

SHEILA JACKSON LEE

A U.S. Representative from Texas, she emerged as a charismatic leader in Congress during the 1998 impeachment hearings. Elected in 1994, in the face of a Republican landslide, she has distinguished herself as a staunch defender of civil rights and African American interests.

CORETTA SCOTT KING

As a partner in the Martin Luther King Jr. story, she has made key contributions to the freedom struggle in her own right, including founding and serving as the longtime head of the King Center for Nonviolent Social Change and leading the charge for a national holiday in honor of her slain husband.

MARY EDMONIA LEWIS (1843?–1890?)

The first major Black woman sculptor, she carved out a place in history with stirring pieces that captured in stone the power and emotion of the African American and Native American experiences.

MOMS MABLEY (1894?–1975)

She was the salty old lady with the tattered clothes, the toothless smile and the bawdy routine that reduced everyone to tears of laughter and shaped the timing and sensibilities of comics to come. Before there was Def Comedy Jam, there was Moms, who appeared more often than any performer at the Apollo Theatre, and whose enduring career stretched from vaudeville to television.

OSEOLA McCARTY

The model of thrift and generosity, this tiny woman earned her keep taking in laundry in Hattiesburg, Miss. She never made much money, but simple living allowed her to amass a nest egg of $150,000, all of which she donated to the University of Southern Mississippi to establish a scholarship fund for Black students.

AUTHERINE LUCY

With quiet dignity and the backing of the NAACP, she smashed through the barriers blocking African Americans from the University of Alabama, becoming the first Black student to enroll there in 1956 and paving the way for the unrest and change that would sweep the nation in the ensuing years.

TERRY McMILLAN

One of the most popular women writers of all time, her phenomenally successful novels, which chart the lives and loves of contemporary Black women, shattered illusions about the book-buying habits of African Americans. Two of her most popular books not only racked up unprecedented sales, but were adapted with equal success into films.

FLORENCE MILLS (1896–1927)

A bundle of talent in a petite package, this extraordinary singer and dancer was the first Black female Broadway star and one of the leading musical comedy performers of the Jazz Age.

CONSTANCE BAKER MOTLEY

The first Black woman federal judge, she also was a member of the historic team of attorneys who won the land-mark Brown v. Board of Education decision that declared an end to legal segregation in the United States.

TONI MORRISON

Novelist and essayist, her commanding and demanding literary style gripped readers throughout the world, enabling her to become the first Black American to win the Nobel Prize for literature. She was cited for her 1986 novel Beloved.

CAROL MOSELEY-BRAUN

The first Black Democratic senator and the first Black woman senator, her 1992 victory helped redefine the role of women in American politics and national leadership.

JESSYE NORMAN

With a voice as grand as her presence, this versatile diva rocketed to the top of the opera world, reinterpreting the most famous roles in the classical repertoire and amazing audiences throughout the United States and Europe with her shimmering vocal technique.

HAZEL O'LEARY

Named Secretary of Energy by President Clinton, she is the first Black woman to hold a cabinet post outside the fields of health, education, welfare and housing.

DOROTHY PORTER (1905–1995)

Librarian and curator, recipient of the Charles Frankel Prize in the Humanities, her tireless efforts to collect artifacts of African American history laid the groundwork for Howard University's Moorland-Spingarn Research Center, one of the largest repositories of Black History in the country. Her work helped gain acceptance for Black studies as an academic discipline.

ROSA PARKS

Often called "The Mother of the Civil Rights Movement," she triggered the Montgomery Bus Boycott when she refused to give up her seat on a Jim Crow bus.

ANN PETRY (1908–1997)

Pioneering novelist, she eloquently evoked the trials and triumphs of urban Black life from a decidedly feminine perspective, breathing new life into the genre and smashing the stereotypes of Black women that dominated the popular culture of her day.

LEONTYNE PRICE

Hailed by critics as the greatest soprano of her era, she was the first Black international diva. Her success paved the way for classical artists such as Kathleen Battle and Jessye Norman.

MA RAINEY (1886–1939)

Dubbed "the Mother of the Blues" she rose from minstrel impresario to become one of the biggest recording stars of her era. Her rich, gravelly voiced brand of Delta blues struck a national chord and still resonates throughout the culture.

WILMA RUDOLPH (1940–1994)

The first woman to win three gold medals in a single Olympiad, she was triumphant in the 100- and 200-meter dashes and the 400-meter relay in 1960.

RACHEL ROBINSON

She was the other half of the team that gave us the first Black player in major league baseball in modern times. She keeps her husband's dream alive as the head of the Jackie Robinson Foundation.

EDITH SAMPSON (1901–1979)

Rose to national prominence in 1950 when Harry Truman appointed her as the first Black delegate to the United Nations. She also was the first Black person to hold an appointment with the North Atlantic Treaty Organization (NATO), the first Black woman appointed a judge in Illinois and the first Black woman to graduate from Chicago's Loyola University Law School.

BETTY SHABAZZ (1936–1997)

Side by side with Malcolm X, she helped forge a new path in the freedom struggle. After her husband's assassination, she became an education administrator and the keeper of his flame.

BESSIE SMITH (1894–1937)

The undisputed "Empress" of the blues was more than an entertainer, she was a cultural force, a towering symbol of Black pride and the rising tide of Black activism circa 1920. She didn't just sing the blues, she spread the message of Black love and Black life, all the while demanding equality.

THE SUPREMES

Young, talented and beautiful, they were the princesses of popular music, dazzling divas-in-the-making whose sweet, soothing harmonies reached across the racial divide and had all of America touching somebody's hand and stopping in the name of love. Individually, they were Mary Wilson, Florence Ballard and Diana Ross. Collectively, they were simply ... Supreme.

MABEL STAUPERS (1890–1989)

Nurse activist who spent her entire life on the front lines, either mending the wounds of men in battle or leading the charge against segregation in the U.S. Army Nurse Corps. Her long campaign, extending from the Great Depression to World War II, resulted in the full integration of Black nurses into the Army and ultimately into civilian hospitals as well.

MARY CHURCH TERRELL (1863–1954)

Educator, civil rights activist and women's rights leader, she advocated advancing all of Black America by improving the lives of African American women. She also was a founding member of the NAACP and the National Association of Colored Women.

SARAH VAUGHAN (1924–1990)

Combining precise phrasing with incredible, yet effortless, range, "The Divine One" scaled seemingly unreachable vocal heights and took jazz singing to an entirely new level.

SUE BAILEY THURMAN (1903–1996)

In partnership with her husband, noted scholar and theologian Howard Thurman, she promoted the spiritual and social uplift of Black Americans. An activist in her own right, she criss-crossed the country preaching the gospel of nonviolent resistance and helped to establish what was believed to be the first integrated church in the United States.

CICELY TYSON

On stage and on screen, she redefined the Black woman— and the White woman—and, in the process, personified the cultural sea change sweeping the country.

ALICE WALKER

A Pulitzer Prize winner in 1983 for The Color Purple, this novelist, essayist, poet and short story writer has been at the forefront of the women's movement for nearly 30 years and remains one its most prolific and influential voices.

DINAH WASHINGTON (1924–1963)

Dubbed "Queen of the Blues," she was, in fact, a rhythm and blues pioneer and a singer of immense versatility. Whether growling out a down-home blues number or purring

120

a cover of some pop hit, she mesmerized audiences and paved the way for the generation of singers who followed.

ETHEL WATERS (1896–1977)

Actress and blues singer, she was a star of the famed Cotton Club in the '20s and the toast of Broadway in the '30s. Later, she established herself in dramatic roles on stage and in films. She won raves and an Academy Award nomination (Pinky), and became one of the highest-paid performers of the '40s and '50s.

MAGGIE LENA WALKER (1867–1934)

The first woman bank president in the United States, she built the Independent Order of St. Luke into one of the most progressive and profitable mutual aid societies of the early 20th century. As executive head of the Richmond-based agency, she presided over its banking and insurance enterprises and was a tireless civic leader.

MAXINE WATERS

The four-term congresswoman from California rose to national prominence as the leading spokeswoman for her Los Angeles district, which was ravaged in the wake of the riots that followed the 1992 acquittal of the four White police officers charged in the Rodney King beating. She has emerged as a passionate advocate for the nation's often neglected inner cities.

FAYE WATTLETON

The former president of the Planned Parenthood Federation of America, she eloquently articulated critical women's issues in the '70s and '80s, and became a leading figure in the women's movement.

VANESSA WILLIAMS

The first Black woman to wear the Miss America crown had her reign abbreviated by scandal in 1984. Yet she rose like a phoenix to conquer Broadway and Hollywood while simultaneously establishing a chart-topping recording career.

Appendix 5

Selecting a Female Role Model

Carefully select a woman to model your life after of. Find someone you respect and admire.

Describe her strengths.

_____
_____
_____
_____
_____
_____
_____

Why did you select her?

_____
_____
_____
_____
_____
_____
_____

Describe her uplifting and inspiring qualities:

_____
_____
_____
_____
_____
_____

Appendix 6

Understanding Abuse

It is important to understand abuse. Some of you are in abusive relationships and do not know it. Love should not hurt; at least not intentionally. I hope you find this information to be helpful.

Different forms of abuse

- Physical Abuse (inflicting physical discomfort, pain or injury) Slapping, hitting, burning, punching, restraining, sexually assaulting, handling roughly, etc.
- Sexual Abuse (forced sexual contact, rape or incest)
- Psychological/emotional abuse (diminishing your identity and self-worth) Threatening, insulting, name calling, yelling, imitating, ignoring, isolating, etc.
- Neglect (failure to meet your needs or those of others) Inadequate physical or emotional care: denial of food, water, clothing, health care, etc.

Symptoms of Abuse — **"Misuse of Power and Control"**

Using Physical Abuse

- Pushed or shoved you
- Held you to keep you from leaving
- Slapped or bit you
- Kicked, choked, hit or punched you
- Locked you out of the house

- Abandoned you in a dangerous place
- Refused to help you when you were sick, injured, or pregnant
- Subjected you to reckless driving
- Forced you off the road or kept you from driving
- Raped you
- Threatened or hurt you with a weapon

Using Sexual Abuse

- Told anti-woman jokes or made demeaning remarks about women
- Insisted that you dress in a more sexual way than you wanted
- Called you derogatory sexual names like "whore" or "freak"
- Forced you to strip when you did not want to
- Forced you to have unwanted sex with others or forced you to watch others
- Forced sex after beatings
- Forced sex for the purpose of hurting you with objects or weapons
- Committed sadistic sexual acts

Using Emotional Abuse

- Put you down
- Made you feel bad about yourself
- Called you names
- Made you think you are crazy
- Played minds games with you
- Humiliated you
- Made you feel guilty

Using Male Privilege

- Treated you like a servant
- Made all the big decisions
- Acted like the "master of the castle"
- Was the one to define men's and women's roles

Using Economic Abuse

- Prevented you from getting or keeping a job
- Made you ask for money
- Gave you an allowance
- Took your money
- Didn't let you know about or have access to family income

Using Coercion and Threats

- Made or carried out threats to do something to hurt you
- Threatened to leave you, to commit suicide, to report you to welfare
- Made you drop charges
- Made you do illegal things

Using Intimidation

- Made you afraid by using looks, gestures, or actions
- Smashed things
- Abused pets
- Displayed weapons

----------------------A Black Woman's Worth!----------------------

Using Children

- Made you feel guilty about the children
- Used the children to relay messages
- Used visitation to harass you
- Threatened to take the children away

Using Isolation

- Controlled what you do, who you see and talk to, what you read and where you go
- Limited your outside involvement
- Used jealousy to justify actions

Minimizing, Denying, Blaming

- Made light of the abuse and did not take your concerns about it seriously
- Said the abuse didn't happen
- Shifted responsibility for abusive behavior
- Said you caused the abuse

Sweet Baby Syndromes (How He Gets To Come Back)

- Honeymoon Syndrome
- Super Dad Syndrome
- Revival Syndrome
- Sobriety Syndrome
- Counseling Syndrome

Common Characteristics of Battered Women

- Has low self-esteem
- Is a traditionalist about the home

- Accepts responsibility for the batterer's actions
- Suffers from guilt, yet denies terror and anger
- Has severe stress reactions with psychophysiological complaints
- Uses sex as a way to establish intimacy
- Believes that no one will be able to help her resolve her predicament

Common Characteristics of the Batterer

- Has low self-esteem
- Believes all the myths about battering relationships
- Is a traditionalist
- Blames others for his actions
- Is pathologically jealous
- Presents a dual personality
- Has severe stress reactions
- Uses sex as an act of aggression
- Does not believe violent behavior should have negative consequences

Reaction of Women Being Beaten

- Denial
- Blaming self
- Ambivalence

Long-Term Effects of Domestic Violence

- Physical
- Mental
- Economic
- Children

Appendix 7

Abuse/Neglect Screening Questionnaire

If you answer yes to one or more of the questions below, please talk to someone you trust and/or seek help.

Has anyone ever touched you without your consent?

Has anyone ever made you do things you didn't want to do?

Has anyone taken anything that was yours without asking?

Has anyone ever scolded or threatened you?

Are you afraid of anyone?

Are you alone a lot?

Do you have low self-esteem?

Do you feel like you are emotionally unstable?

Do you feel depressed? Are you anxious frequently? Are you angry often?

Do you feel hopelessness? Do you feel guilty? Are you sad?

Are you overly compliant or passive?

Are you extremely aggressive or demanding?

Are you extremely dependent on someone else?

**Seek help immediately if you or someone you love is
being abused.**

Battered Women's National Hotline: 1-800-799-7233

Abuse Hotline: 1-888-743-5754

Appendix 8

Strength Inventory

List at least nine personal strengths and review them daily to empower yourself.

1.) _____
2.) _____
3.) _____
4.) _____
5.) _____
6.) _____
7.) _____
8.) _____
9.) _____

As the old saying goes, if it does not kill you it will make you stronger. Learn to focus on your strengths for inspiration. Resiliency is achieved by demonstrating the ability to move forward after experiencing sustained or prolonged trauma or difficulty.

Note Page

Note Page

Scheduling For Seminars, Speaking Engagements or Film Screenings

Dr. Buckingham conducts seminars, speaking engagements and film screenings for groups, churches, and organizations throughout the year.

"A Black Woman's Worth" is one of the most requested seminars; however, Dr. Buckingham conducts seminars and speaks on a variety of topics related to relationship difficulty, stress management, team building and personal growth.

RHCS is dedicated to expanding the horizons of all humans!

To book Dr. Buckingham for your next event:

R.E.A.L. Horizons Consulting Service, LLC
P.O. Box 2665
Silver Spring, MD 20915

240-242-4087 Voice Mail
www.realhorizonsdlb.com

I hope this book has been a blessing to you and I welcome your comments.
dwayne@realhorizonsdlb.com

--------------------A Black Woman's Worth!----------------------

This book can also be purchased on-line at:

www.realhorizonsdlb.com

Amazon.com

Borders.com

BarnesandNoble.com

BooksaMillion.com

About the Author

Dwayne L. Buckingham, Ph.D., LCSW, BCD, is a psychotherapist, film producer and the Founder and Chief Executive Officer of R.E.A.L. Horizons Consulting Service, LLC in Silver Spring, Maryland. A commissioned officer in the United States Air Force, for nearly a decade he provided psychological assessments and treatment to over ten thousand individuals, couples, groups, and families worldwide. Dr. Buckingham currently serves as a Commander in the United States Public Health Service and provides individual and marital therapy to military troops assigned to the Walter Reed National Military Medical Center in Bethesda, Maryland. Also, he is an active member of the National Association of Social Workers and Kappa Alpha Psi Fraternity, Inc.

Dr. Buckingham conducts seminars for groups, families, organizations, and churches each year. Please visit his website at www.realhorizonsdlb.com for more information.

www.ingramcontent.com/pod-product-compliance
Lightning Source LLC
LaVergne TN
LVHW011239080426
835509LV00005B/557